ON TOLERANCE

On Tolerance

A Defence of Moral Independence

FRANK FUREDI

continuum

Published by the Continuum International Publishing Group

The Tower Building	80 Maiden Lane
11 York Road	Suite 704
London	New York
SE1 7NX	NY 10038

www.continuumbooks.com

First published 2011

British Library Cataloguing-in-Publication Data
A catalogue record for this book is available from the British Library.

ISBN: 978-1-4411-2010-6 (HB)

Typeset by Pindar NZ, Auckland, New Zealand
Printed and bound in India

Contents

Preface

Tolerance has been turned into a Hurrah Word, and emptied of its moral and intellectual meaning. The widespread celebration of tolerance in public statements and declarations is testimony to its rhetorical appeal, even as it becomes decreasingly significant as a moral principle for guiding official and public behaviour. The aim of this book is to argue the case for tolerance as a virtue in its own right. Tolerance requires both intellectual justification and cultural support. The capacity to tolerate requires that society takes freedom seriously; tolerating beliefs and views that are hostile to our own requires a degree of confidence in our own convictions, but also the disposition to take risks.

Tolerance is in danger of becoming denuded of its vital freedom-affirming meaning, and is instead frequently interpreted as a form of polite etiquette that offers its recipient respect and validation. Whereas the classical liberal interpretation of tolerance required conviction and judgement, today it frequently conveys the idea of respectful indifference. This book argues, first, that the reinterpretation of the meaning of the term 'tolerance' has created a situation where the principle is taken far less seriously. The second point emphasized is that, the rhetoric of tolerance notwithstanding, contemporary society is afflicted by a powerful sensibility of intolerance. More energy is devoted towards the project of inventing new limits on tolerance than on extending it to new domains of human experience. The third and most important claim argued here is that the cultural values that dominate our lives find it difficult to sustain and uphold true tolerance: indeed, many of the prevailing cultural norms actually negate it.

Historically, intolerance is associated with religious and doctrinal fanaticism. The classical expressions of intolerance are laws against blasphemy, slander, libel and subversion. These classical manifestations of intolerance still survive as moral zealots attempt to protect their traditions and way of life from competing beliefs and secular lifestyles. However, in recent decades a new species of intolerance has become increasingly powerful. These days, calls for banning speech, policing thought and controlling behaviour often come from people who identify themselves as left of centre, open-minded and secular. It is the exploration of this very distinct contemporary manifestation of intolerance that constitutes the focus of this book. Why? Because with the expansion of intolerance across the political divide it is urgent to build a coalition of open-minded people who are genuinely inspired by the ideal of freedom, moral independence and democracy and who are prepared to uphold tolerance without equivocation.

This is not a philosophical text, whose objective is the exploration of the rights and wrongs of intolerance, or which assesses the different theories of toleration. The question that motivated this book is: why has tolerance lost its way? Finding answers to this question is crucial for the workings of a future-oriented, open society. This book is directed towards people who are genuinely open-minded and are prepared to engage with new experience. Tolerance requires consistency and strong convictions regarding at least one moral principle – freedom.

This book has benefitted from the comments and criticism of friends and colleagues. In different ways Jennie Bristow, Brendan O'Neill and Wendy Kaminer helped clarify some of the arguments; of course they bear no responsibility for any of the book's faults. This book is dedicated to my father, Laszlo Furedi. Despite his best effort, he helped me understand that what matters is not simply what you believe but your commitment for taking responsibility.

1

Introduction:
Clarifying the Issues

The idea of tolerance has been subject to significant conceptual confusions. Tolerance is often represented as a form of non-judgemental acceptance of other people's beliefs; yet, to tolerate a disagreeable opinion requires a prior act of judgement. In a world where acceptance of difference is represented as mandatory, the classical idea of tolerance has become problematic. It has either been rejected as far too negative or reinterpreted as a gesture of non-judgemental respect. Through examining the current reaction to tolerance, this introduction sets the scene for a review of its historical evolution.

Controversies over 'gays in the military', the wearing of the burka or the crucifix, or even whether it should be permissible to make offensive comments about someone's culture, indicate that twenty-first-century Western society has an uneasy relationship with the idea and practice of tolerance. As I write I receive a press release from a British think tank announcing that 'wearing the veil is a civil right' and insisting that 'British tolerance' means recognizing 'freedom of religious expression'. In America, too, the age-old question of religious tolerance is the subject of debate. On the eve of 11 September 2010, President Barack Obama felt it necessary to remind the public of the necessity for religious tolerance, after a Florida-based Christian clergyman threatened to burn the Koran in protest against plans to build an Islamic centre two blocks from the site where the World Trade Center stood before its destruction. Some claim that tolerance has gone 'too far', and blame the culture of permissiveness in Western societies for a bewildering variety of social and moral problems, from pornography to the disintegration of the traditional family.

This book argues that, despite its frequent rhetorical use, twenty-first-century society does not take the classical liberal ideal of tolerance very seriously. Even its advocates practise their tolerance selectively, often legitimizing attitudes and behaviour that are censorious and unforgiving towards beliefs and views that challenge their assumptions. Matters are made worse by the confusions that surround the meaning of 'tolerance': the term finds itself used in ways that would shock the philosophers and thinkers who developed this concept. Here, we aim to clarify and elaborate the meaning of tolerance for the current era.

Tolerance is an important ideal that is indispensable for the working of a genuinely free and democratic society. Yet it is an ideal that we take for granted. Numerous articles and books on the subject treat it as a rather insignificant idea that doesn't go far enough to secure a just society. Others depict tolerance as a disinclination to judge or to have strong views about the behaviour of others, or deploy 'tolerance' as a synonym for 'permissive'. Increasingly, we are in danger of forgetting that tolerance is an intimate companion of liberty and freedom, and that it constitutes one of the most precious contributions of the Enlightenment imagination to modern life. Without tolerance we cannot be free, we cannot live with one another in relative peace, we cannot follow and act on our conscience, we cannot exercise our moral autonomy nor pursue our own road towards seeking the truth.

In historical terms, tolerance is a very recent cultural and moral ideal. Until the seventeenth century the toleration of different religions, opinions and beliefs was interpreted as a form of moral cowardice, if not a symptom of heresy. Indeed medieval witch-hunters and inquisitors were no less concerned with stigmatizing those who questioned their intolerant practices than they were with hunting down witches and heretics. The fifteenth-century witch-hunters' manual *Malleus Maleficarum* claimed that those who denied the existence of witches or questioned the methods of the inquisitors were as guilty of heresy as the active practitioners of witchcraft. In the following century, scepticism was frequently treated as a particularly dangerous form of anti-Christian heresy. As the French historian Paul Hazard notes in his pioneering study *The European Mind*, until the seventeenth century tolerance 'had not been a virtue at all, but, on the contrary, a sign of weakness, not to say cowardice', and 'duty and charity' forbade people to be tolerant.[1] As late as 1691, the French theologian Jacques-Bénigne Bossuet boasted that Catholicism was the least tolerant of all religions, stating that 'I have the right to persecute you because I am right and you are wrong'.[2] Protestant religious figures more than matched Bossuet's intolerance. Indeed the Walloon synod of Leyden, mainly composed of Huguenot refugees, condemned religious toleration as a form of heresy.[3]

It was in the seventeenth century that attitudes towards tolerating competing ideas and religions began to change. In part the rise of secularism and rationality encouraged a more sceptical orientation towards religious dogmatism and intolerance. Although there are some historical exceptions, people are far less likely to impose their beliefs on others when they are not

absolutely certain of their convictions. This was also a period
when Europe was overwhelmed by bitter religious conflicts that
frequently resulted in bloody civil wars. In such circumstances,
calls for tolerance were influenced by the pragmatic calculation that without a measure of religious toleration, endemic
violence and bloodshed could not be avoided. This was the
moment when a significant minority of Europeans recognized
that tolerance was a prerequisite for their society's survival.
The American philosopher Michael Walzer emphasizes the
significance of this insight when he states that toleration 'sus-
tains life itself': we need to remind ourselves that 'toleration
makes difference possible; difference makes toleration necessary'.[4] From this perspective toleration is not only a moral or
philosophical principle, but also a matter of pragmatic necessity. It is precisely because many differences cannot be resolved
philosophically that tolerance becomes the only alternative to
conflict and violence.

The aim of seventeenth-century advocates of tolerance,
including John Locke, was to protect religious belief from
state coercion. Locke's advocacy of toleration represented a
call for restraining political authorities from interfering with
the workings of individual conscience and lifestyles. Over the
centuries this affirmation of religious tolerance has expanded
to allow the free expression of opinions, beliefs and behaviour associated with the exercise of the individual conscience.
Tolerance is intimately connected to the assertion of this most
basic dimension of freedom, and demands that we accept the
right of people to live according to beliefs and opinions that are
different, sometimes antithetical, to ours. Tolerance does not
invite us to accept or celebrate other people's sentiments, but
requires that we live with them and desist from interfering or
forcing others to fall in line with our own views. As Murphy

writes, 'neither conceptually nor historically is toleration affiliated with approval of diversity or with intellectual, religious, or moral pluralism *per se*'.[5]

In this book the concept of tolerance is used in two senses. It pertains to the domain of the political/philosophical through its avowal of the principle of non-interference towards the way that people develop and hold beliefs and opinions. Tolerance affirms the freedom of conscience and individual autonomy. As long as an act does not violate a person's moral autonomy and harm others, tolerance also calls for the absence of constraint on behaviour linked to the exercise of individual autonomy. From this perspective, tolerance can be measured in relation to the extent to which people's belief and behaviour is not subject to institutional and political interference and restraint. Second, tolerance is a social/cultural accomplishment, and a tolerant society is one where the cultural orientation discourages and restrains social intolerance. This was a concern eloquently pursued by the philosopher J. S. Mill, who warned about the 'tyranny' of public opinion and its tendency to stigmatize and silence minority and dissident beliefs. Upholding the disposition to be tolerant is always a challenge, and experience shows that legal safeguards can always come unstuck when confronted by a tidal wave of social intolerance.

What tolerance is not

Anyone perusing policy documents, mission statements, school textbooks and speeches made by politicians and policymakers is likely to be struck by the frequency with which the term 'tolerance' is celebrated. It is difficult to encounter any significant acclaim for intolerance. However, on closer inspection it becomes evident that the meaning of this term has radically altered, mutating into a superficial signifier of acceptance and affirmation. In official documents and school texts, tolerance is used as a desirable character trait rather than as a way of managing conflicting beliefs and behaviour. So one can be tolerant without any reference to a set of beliefs or opinions. Moreover, the idea that tolerance means not interfering with, or attempting to suppress, beliefs that contradict one's own sentiments has given way to the idea that tolerance involves not judging other people and their views. Instead of serving as a way of responding to differences of views, tolerance has become a way of not taking them seriously.

When tolerance is represented as a form of detached indifference or as a polite gesture connoting mechanical acceptance, it becomes a vice rather than a virtue. One reason why tolerance was historically interpreted as a virtue was because it implied a willingness to tolerate disagreeable beliefs and opinions. According to the classical liberal outlook, it involved an act of judgement and discrimination; but judgement did not serve as a prelude to censoring another person's wrong views, because tolerance demands respect for people's right to hold beliefs in accordance with their conscience. Indeed, the recognition of the primacy of freedom imposed on the truly tolerant the responsibility to refrain from attempting to coerce religious and political opponents into silence. Voltaire's frequently repeated statement, 'I disapprove of what you say, but I will defend to the death your right to say it', expressed the intimate connection between judgement/disapproval and a commitment to freedom. The capacity to tolerate views of which one disapproves is underpinned by the conviction that this virtue provides an opportunity for testing out ideas and confronting ethical dilemmas. Interference with individual belief and opinion disrupts the creative dynamic of intellectual and moral development of society. From this standpoint, tolerance of disapproved-of beliefs is a very small price to pay for society's intellectual and moral development.

In contemporary public discussion, the connection between tolerance and judgement is in danger of being lost. Our analysis of the current usage of the word 'tolerant' indicates that it is frequently used as a companion term with 'inclusive' and 'non-judgemental'. As a fascinating survey of American political culture concludes, 'Thou shalt not judge' has become the eleventh commandment of middle-class Americans. Alan Wolfe, the study's author, notes that 'middle-class Americans are reluctant to pass judgement on how other people act and think'.[6] While the reluctance to judge other people's behaviour has its attractive qualities, it is not necessarily a manifestation of social tolerance. All too often this attitude is synonymous with not caring about the fate of others. Yet the precondition for the working of a democratic public sphere is openness to conversation and debate. Reflecting on our differences with others' points of view, letting them know where we stand and what we find disagreeable in their opinions, is the very stuff of a vibrant democracy. Without it tolerance turns into shallow indifference, an excuse for switching off when others talk.

The confusion of the concept of tolerance with the idea of acceptance and valuation of other people's beliefs and lifestyles is strikingly illustrated by the United Nations Educational, Scientific and Cultural Organization (UNESCO) Declaration on the Principles of Tolerance, which frames the term thus: 'tolerance is respect, acceptance and appreciation of the rich diversity of our world's cultures, our forms of expression and ways of being human' and it is 'harmony in difference'.[7] For UNESCO toleration becomes an expansive and diffuse sensibility that automatically accepts and offers unconditional appreciation of different views and cultures. This officially sanctioned declaratory rhetoric of tolerance is often used in schools, and children interpret it as an exhortation to be nice to other people. Children are taught that a nice person is a tolerant one, and tolerance is diagnosed as a psychological trait – a variant of other fashionable pedagogic values such as empathy, self-esteem, or valuing yourself.

The reinterpretation of tolerance as a psychological attitude that conveys acceptance, empathy and respect means that in public deliberations it has lost its real meaning. Yet it is precisely the intimate connection between disapproval/disagreement and toleration that endows tolerance with the potential to enhance the quality of public life. The act of toleration demands reflection, restraint and a respect for the right of other people to find their way to their truth. Once tolerance signifies a form of automatic acceptance, it becomes a performance in expected behaviour. As David Heyd writes, the shift in meaning, 'which rests on easy acceptance of the heterogeneity of values and ways of life', pushes 'the concept of tolerance dangerously close to that of indifference'. The 'scope of indifference is growing in the field of value judgments, and . . . liberalism today means less the toleration of other ways of life than the cool acceptance of the very plurality and heterogeneity of lifestyles'.[8] So inadvertently well-meaning exhortations to tolerate discourage people from developing their moral capacity to understand, judge and discriminate. In education where tolerance is represented as an attitude to be learned, it becomes 'detached from affirming any moral views'.[9]

The detachment of toleration from any specific object has encouraged a widely practised pedagogy that instructs children to 'tolerate diversity' or 'tolerate difference'. Such pedagogy self-consciously avoids encouraging children to develop their capacity for moral reasoning or the making of moral judgements. However, descriptive terms like 'difference' or 'diversity' possess no intrinsic moral qualities – they are some of the conditions of life within which reasoning, including moral reflection, occurs. When tolerance becomes disassociated from a reflection of contrasting beliefs and opinions, children are protected from troubling themselves with the challenge of engaging with moral dilemmas. In such circumstances, tolerance becomes a colloquial idiom for approval.

The call to reinterpret tolerance as a sentiment conveying non-judgementalism or indifference is often presented as a positive character trait of the open-minded person. But the gesture of affirmation and acceptance can be seen as a way of avoiding making difficult moral choices and of disengaging from the complicated challenge of explaining the values that have to be upheld. It is far easier to dispense with the idea of moral judgement than to explain why a certain way of life is preferable to the one that should be tolerated but not embraced.

Tolerance has also been adapted by well-meaning national and international agencies and institutions as an adjective that conveys the sense of harmony and peacefulness. Not infrequently it is depicted as the polar opposite to conflict. The UNESCO Declaration on Tolerance is paradigmatic in this respect. Its call for tolerance is presented as a response to

the current rise in acts of intolerance, violence, terrorism, xenophobia, aggressive nationalism, racism, anti-Semitism, exclusion, marginalization and discrimination directed against national, ethnic, religious and linguistic minorities, refugees, migrant workers, immigrants and vulnerable groups within societies, as well as acts of violence and intimidation committed against individuals exercising their freedom of opinion and expression – all of which threaten the consolidation of peace and democracy, both nationally and internationally, and are obstacles to development.[10]

Presenting this shopping list of ills that afflict the world as an argument for tolerance has a purely rhetorical quality. It is based on the strategy of branding intolerance as the cause of all forms of dangerous conflicts. However, intolerance is far more likely to be one of the many expressions of a particular conflict than its cause. It requires a formidable capacity for conceptual juggling to recycle intolerance as a generic cause of conflict and represent tolerance as its antidote.

The representation of tolerance as an antidote to a variety of group conflicts represents an understandable but unhelpful expansion of the meaning of tolerance. As the American political philosopher Wendy Brown observes, 'coined in early modern Europe to deal with religious dissent and the eruption of individual claims of conscience against church and state authority, tolerance now takes as its object a wide array of differences, including sexuality, ethnicity, race, nationality, and subnationality, as well as religious affiliation'.[11] The reorientation of tolerance from personal beliefs to group identities and conflicts does not simply mean its quantitative expansion, but a qualitative transformation in meaning. Tolerance has a different meaning when addressed towards religious beliefs and political opinions that express 'individual moral understanding' than when it is directed towards 'attributes or identities taken to be given, saturating, and immutable'.[12]

The tendency to perceive differences in group and cultural terms distracts attention from conflicts of belief and opinion. However, it is important to understand that toleration pertains to beliefs and behaviour, rather than to differences in cultural or national identities. Everyone who upholds liberty will adopt a liberal and open-minded approach towards the right of all people to be who they are, but the recognition of this right has little to do with the classical ideal of tolerance. In such circumstances what is called for is the affirmation of the democratic right to equal treatment.

The term tolerance can be used to signify an approach towards a person and a group insofar as it pertains to beliefs and opinions and forms of behaviour linked to them. So, tolerating Protestants, Muslims or Jews pertains not to their DNA, or their cultural or national identity but to their beliefs and the rituals and practices associated with them. Unfortunately, in contemporary society, differences in views are invariably represented as a cultural accomplishment rather than as linked to individual conscience or moral reasoning. According to this perspective, belief is not so much the outcome of reflection, conscience, revelation or discovery as it is an attribute of identity. As Brown notes, according to the current paradigm of tolerance, 'opinions, belief, and practices are cast not as matters of conscience, education, or revelation but as the material of the person of which certain attributes (racial, sexual, gendered, or ethnic) are an index': hence notions of 'black consciousness', 'women's morality', 'queer sensibility' and 'cultural viewpoint'.[13] One important consequence of this shift in emphasis is that beliefs and opinions acquire the fetishistic form of a cultural value that is fixed and not susceptible to a genuine conversation. In such circumstances toleration can only mean an acceptance of the fossilization of difference.

Critics of the classical ideal of tolerance insist that in the current era this concept is defective for managing the conflicts between groups and cultural identities. After observing that 'what gives rise to most genuine contemporary issues of toleration are, in fact, differences between groups rather than individuals', Galeotti remarks that such group conflicts are more problematic for tolerance to handle since 'group differences normally have an ascriptive nature, in that, unlike the cases discussed by classical theorists of toleration they do not involve choice'.[14] However, in this case the problem is not with the concept of tolerance but its inappropriate extension to situations to which it is not suitable. Just because it is not suitable for the task of managing group conflict, it does not follow that tolerance does not retain its vital role of protecting people's beliefs and political views.

Historically, laws concerning religious toleration emerged before other forms of democratic freedoms were recognized. But it is essential to understand that tolerance is not only chronologically but also logically prior to the working of freedom and liberty. If people are not allowed to hold their own beliefs and act in accordance with them, their very potential for exercising their moral autonomy becomes compromised.

Tolerance under attack

Outwardly, we live in an era that appears more open-minded, non-judgemental and tolerant that at any time in human history. The very term 'intolerant' invokes moral condemnation. Time and again the public is instructed in the importance of respecting diversity and different cultures. Students are frequently reminded that there is no such thing as a right answer and that there are many truths. Those with strong beliefs are often dismissed as fundamentalists or zealots. Yet the language of open-minded liberalism exists in an uneasy relation with censorious and intolerant attitudes towards those causing moral outrage. That policymakers and politicians can so casually demand 'zero tolerance' indicates that at the very least society is selective about how it applies the principle of tolerance. Zero tolerance can be understood as a cultural metaphor that prescribes an indiscriminate template response to different forms of undesirable behaviour. Initially, zero tolerance was invoked as the threat of an automatic punishment for certain forms of criminal behaviour and legal infraction. Since the 1990s the policy of zero tolerance has been expanded into the school system to refer to acts of bullying, harassment, possessing drugs or weapons. In the UK public sector it is common to come across posters that warn of zero tolerance of aggressive behaviour towards members of staff. In recent times, the term has been adopted by politicians, opinion-makers and business people to communicate the idea that they feel strongly that the target of their concern should be suppressed: so a director of the Association of British Insurers felt able to call for 'zero tolerance towards fraud'.[15] The casual way with which zero tolerance policies, which serve as warrants for intolerance, are affirmed expresses the shallow cultural support enjoyed by the ideal of tolerance.

The term 'zero tolerance policy' conveys the idea that its author means business. It also calls into question the cultural and human qualities that are usually associated with the capacity to tolerate. As social commentator Bruce Schneier reminds us, 'these so-called zero-tolerance policies are actually zero-discretion policies'.[16] These are policies that are meant to be applied arbitrarily and punish without regard to circumstances, sparing judges and officials from having to think about the circumstances affecting a particular event and from exercising their capacity to discriminate. The abolition of discretion reflects a general unease with the act of judgement: yet judgement and discrimination are essential qualities for developing both the disposition to tolerate and an understanding of what form of behaviour cannot be tolerated. Non-judgementalism is therefore a value that is upheld not only by the advocates of tolerance but also by promoters of zero tolerance. Their joint hostility towards discretion indicates that they may have more in common than they suspect.

Tolerance has always been very selectively elaborated, conceptualized and applied. From the outset its advocates believed in the toleration of some views but not others. Throughout the seventeenth century, religious leaders, philosophers and political leaders tended to promote toleration opportunistically and tactically. This tendency continues to this day. During the course of a debate in Amsterdam I encountered people who agreed that there should be tolerance towards people prepared to criticize Islam, but that there should be zero tolerance towards deniers of the Holocaust. I have also had the pleasure of arguing with people who argue the reverse, insisting that while it is tolerable to question the existence of gas chambers in Auschwitz, any blasphemy directed towards the Koran should be banned.

The double standard that afflicts discussions around the Holocaust or Islam is evident in relation to a variety of subjects, even in the serious academic literature on the subject. Somehow abstract philosophical explorations of the tensions contained within tolerance conclude by taking sides. Indeed it is difficult to avoid the conclusion that such philosophical enquiries are far from disinterested studies of the application of the idea of tolerance to contemporary debates about identity politics, lifestyle controversies, or the right of free speech to offend. They often represent a plea for tolerating or respecting groups and views that they uphold and for adopting an intolerant stance towards those that they condemn. The Italian political philosopher Anna Galeotti insists that minorities do not just need to be tolerated but also respected, whereas those who use 'hate speech' against them can be censored and silenced. 'It is argued that the restriction of some people's liberty is necessary to allow for the full toleration of differences which are the target of discrimination and prejudice', she contends.[17]

The regularity with which double standards are applied towards tolerance indicates that such inconsistency is not simply a symptom of moral opportunism. It also reveals the absence of a robust system of cultural support for genuine toleration. Indeed it is striking how the official exhortation to be tolerant appears to lack significant intellectual and moral support. With some important honourable exceptions, academics and social commentators do not appear to take tolerance very seriously. Often tolerance is casually dismissed as an ideal that was important in the past but has become ever so yesterday. It is represented as a necessary but passive act of putting up with someone else's view, and because the act of toleration involves putting up with views deemed wrong or inferior it is seen as having a fundamentally negative connotation. 'Because of tolerance's negative connotations, it is frequently rejected as a political principle in favour of loftier ideas of equality, liberty, or respect', writes one thoughtful commentator on this subject.[18]

Noting that in 'many circles, toleration has a negative image', the Australian political scientist Peter Balint writes that 'it is associated with either mere toleration (as opposed to some sort of enthusiastic acceptance or respect), and also with the necessary association of a negative value'.[19] The idea that 'mere toleration' is not enough or is even disrespectful is fuelled by a cultural sensibility that is deeply uncomfortable with the act of criticizing other people's versions of the truth. Indeed one way of freeing tolerance from having a negative image is by disassociating it from critical judgement.

The claim that tolerance is not enough is often associated with the argument that it is not a suitable principle for managing conflicts between different individuals and groups in contemporary society. For example Islamic studies professor Tariq Ramadan is prepared to accept that tolerance had some value in the distant past, but contends that it no longer possesses any positive virtues:

> What was once an act of resistance in the face of powers (which can also be represented by the majority, the elite, the rich, and so on), and a brave, determined call inviting them to be tolerant, changes its meaning and import when we are dealing with equal relationships between free human beings, relations between the citizens of civil society, or even relations between different cultures and civilizations.[20]

According to this argument, tolerance has lost its positive content because it no longer involves the questioning of power. Consequently, Ramadan portrays the call for tolerance as expressing acquiescence to prevailing power relations. 'Calling upon powers to be tolerant once meant asking them to moderate their strength and to limit their ability to do harm: this actually implied an acceptance of a power relationship that might exist between the State and individuals, the police and citizens, or between colonizers and the colonized', he writes.[21]

It is important to recall that the call for toleration by liberals like Locke or Mill was not motivated by the objective of challenging relations of power but by the goal of restraining the state from regulating people's views and opinions. This outlook was motivated by the impulse of upholding the freedom of belief, conscience and speech, because liberals took the view that it was preferable for people to find their own path to the truth than that truth should be imposed from above.[22] It was how the power of the state was used, rather than power relations in general, which the demand for toleration sought to address. However, Ramadan's principal motive for questioning the virtue of tolerance seems to be less his commitment to questioning the prevailing relations of power than his objection to the acts of judgement, evaluation and discrimination, which are integral to the act of tolerance.

Ramadan regards toleration as a form of paternalism towards the objects of their tolerance, castigating tolerance as the 'intellectual charity' of the powerful. Indeed from this perspective this act constitutes an insult, since 'when standing on equal footing, one does not expect to be merely tolerated or grudgingly accepted'.[23] In an era where acceptance and affirmation have acquired the status of a default gesture towards other people, tolerance can readily be interpreted as patronizing or simply not enough. It is frequently argued that people 'do not want to be subject to the negative valuation that tolerance necessarily seems to carry with it'. According to the philosopher John Horton, people want more than toleration: 'the demand for more than mere tolerance is the demand that what one is or does no longer be the object of the negative valuation that is an essential ingredient of toleration'.[24]

The statement that people do not want to be tolerated is another way of stating that not only do they not want to be judged – they also want to be affirmed. Western culture's dissonance regarding tolerance is further reinforced by its celebration of the therapeutic value of affirmation and self-esteem. As noted in Chapter 4, the affirmation of individual and group identity is frequently presented as a sacred duty. It is precisely the contradiction between toleration and affirmation that fosters an inhospitable cultural climate for the practice of tolerance. One strategy for overcoming this contradiction is to expand the meaning of tolerance to encompass the idea of acceptance and respect. Galeotti argues along these lines for a 'general revision of the concept of toleration'. What she proposes is the transformation of the meaning of tolerance so that it communicates the act of recognition: 'toleration will be conceived as a form of recognition of different identities in the public sphere', through what she describes as a 'semantic extension from the negative meaning of non-interference to the positive sense of acceptance and recognition'.[25] This semantic extension of the concept to encompass the idea of uncritical recognition transforms its very meaning to that of unconditional acceptance.

Ramadan also upholds the value of recognition and respect, but because he is far more consistent than Galeotti he rejects the concept of tolerance altogether. Instead of giving tolerance a new meaning he seeks to consign it to the vocabulary of cultural domination, insisting that 'when it comes to relations between free and equal human beings, autonomous and independent nations, or civilizations, religions and cultures, appeals for the tolerance of others are no longer relevant'. Why? Because, 'when we are on equal terms, it is no longer a matter of *conceding* tolerance, but of rising above that and educating ourselves to respect others'.[26] In passing it is worth noting that the liberal idea of tolerance also upholds the notion of respect: not the unconditional affirmation transmitted by today's anti-judgemental idiom of respect, but the liberal notion of possessing respect for people's potential for exercising moral autonomy.

It is important to understand that calls for respect and

recognition do not simply mean an exhortation to be polite and sensitive to the beliefs, cultures and predicament of other people. It often expresses disenchantment with people's capacity to exercise moral agency. As we note in Chapter 5, the provision of unconditional recognition is based on the belief that individuals and groups are disposed towards psychological harm unless they are routinely affirmed. This is based on the premise that people lack the intellectual and moral resources to cope with conflicting opinions. Critics of tolerance are particularly sceptical about the very exercise of individual autonomy. Herbert Marcuse, in his well-known radical-left critique of tolerance, argued that the 'false consciousness' of the people made it difficult if not impossible for them to choose between competing values and arguments. Wendy Brown echoes Marcuse's scepticism regarding the exercise of individual autonomy, warning that the free exercise of conscience may well be illusory. 'What makes choices "freer" when they are constrained by secular and market organizations of femininity and fashion rather than by state or religious law?', she asks.[27] In other words, what's the use of legal toleration if people's ability to make choices is circumscribed by the influence of market forces and institutions such as advertising and cultural norms?

Brown collapses the ideas of formal and social freedom, and refuses to recognize the importance of the former. Formal freedom is not just an empty right: the non-interference of the state in the domain of belief and opinion gives people the freedom to choose their truth in line with their selves. It does not provide a guarantee that people will be able to exercise that freedom in line with their personal interests or individual conscience; but just because a formal freedom does not inexorably lead to the realization of an individual's desires does not render it unimportant. It merely signifies that tolerance provides the precondition for the exercise of freedom, rather than a guarantee of its realization.

Some critics of tolerance denounce it for thwarting people's aspiration for recognition and for fooling them into thinking that they are free. Brown states that tolerance 'appears' in a way that hides the 'inequality and the regulation' of its subjects. She appears to believe that the assumption of tolerance represents an act of unwarranted moral superiority, writing that in its relation to non-liberal cultures 'liberalism acquires moral superiority through its ability to tolerate in its midst those thought not to be able to tolerate liberalism in their midst'.[28] The conviction that a tolerant society is preferable to one that eschews tolerance inevitably expresses a contrast between a superior and an inferior way of managing human affairs. However, the refusal to make such a value judgement is tantamount to refusing to take freedom and liberty seriously.

Wendy Brown characterizes tolerance as a 'discourse of depoliticization'. Although she recognizes that historically toleration had some redeeming features, she is critical of the way that the discourse of tolerance has become an instrument for the legitimation of diverse forms of oppressive domination such as the 'legitimation of a new form of imperial state action'.[29] She argues that 'tolerance discourse in the United States, while posing as both universal value and an impartial practice, designates certain beliefs and practices as civilized and others as barbaric'.[30] On the cover of Brown's book, the well-known American academic Stanley Fish points out the 'inability of liberals to see the dark side of their favourite virtue'.[31] From this standpoint tolerance is seen as best a cynical compromise.

Not only postmodernist and leftist intellectuals feel uncomfortable with upholding tolerance. Many conservative and right-wing thinkers mistake tolerance for licence or lack of moral restraint, confusing the official depiction of tolerance as the routine acknowledgement of difference, conflicting views and behaviours, with its legitimate meaning. Consequently, they frequently blame tolerance for the ascendancy of values, lifestyles and forms of behaviour that they find abhorrent. Writing in this vein, Christopher Caldwell blames the advocacy of tolerance for undermining European cultural identity through the promotion of mass immigration into the continent:

> In the name of liberal universalism, many of the laws and customs that had held European societies together were thrown out the window. Tolerance became a higher priority than any of the traditional preoccupations of state and society – order, liberty, fairness, and intelligibility – and came to be pursued at their expense. But in recent years Europe's ideology of neutrality has buckled under the weight of mass immigration and become a source not of strength but of what Alsana, the bitchy Bengali housewife in Zadie Smith's *White Teeth*, called 'hosh-kosh nonsense'.[32]

Whereas Ramadan decries tolerance for not offering unconditional affirmation for the new immigrant communities of Europe, Caldwell blames tolerance for being too accepting of competing values and norms. The main difference between Caldwell and Ramadan is that the former is concerned about the loss of identity of the tolerator, whereas the latter is concerned about the status of the tolerated.

Opponents of the liberal idea of tolerance insist that they aspire to something that is more elevated or progressive than the gesture of mere toleration. Often they insist that the classical concept of tolerance is too negative and what they propose is a more positive version of this ideal. Former Taoiseach of

Ireland, Garrett Fitzgerald, recalled that for him the word toleration 'still carries echoes of at best grudging acceptance, and at worst ill-disguised hostility', which is why he wants a more positive term that affirms 'human solidarity'.[33] The German philosopher Karl-Otto Apel argues that negative tolerance is not sufficient to deal with the challenges faced by a multicultural society, and calls for the embrace of 'positive or affirmative tolerance' which respects and 'even' supports a 'variety of value traditions'.[34]

The claim that the classical ideal of tolerance is merely a negative one is based on misunderstanding the dialectic of tolerance and disapproval. An example of this confusion is provided by Galeotti, when she writes that 'if they could, tolerant people would wish the tolerated behaviour out of existence'.[35] The argument that given half a chance the tolerant would rather get rid of views of which he or she disapproves misunderstands the meaning of tolerance. The act of tolerance is not a grudgingly extended altruistic gesture, nor does it simply mean deciding to live with behaviour and sentiment that one disapproves. It represents a positive appreciation of the necessity for a diversity of views and for conflicting beliefs. As Mill noted, individual autonomy can only flourish when exposed to a variety of opinions, beliefs and lifestyles. Tolerance represents a positive orientation towards creating the conditions where people can develop their autonomy through the freedom to make choices.

Critics of so-called negative tolerance not only overlook its liberating potential: through failing to take this ideal seriously they often become accomplices to projects of intolerance. Once tolerance is regarded as an instrumental act of indifference to views and opinions the upholding of the freedom of belief and speech ceases to have any intrinsic virtue. That is why Herbert

Marcuse, in his critique of what he characterized as 'repressive tolerance', could effortlessly make a leap from his denunciation of capitalist cultural domination to calling for the suppression of views that he found objectionable. He had no problems with the 'withdrawal of toleration of speech and assembly from groups and movements which promote aggressive policies' or 'discrimination on the grounds of race and religion, or which oppose the extension of public services, social security, medical care'.[36]

As we will see, numerous contemporary critics of 'negative' tolerance follow Marcuse's path and end up arguing for a selective approach towards tolerance, finding themselves elaborating some inventive arguments for policing speech and censoring views that they find abhorrent. In such circumstances, developing a consistent and genuinely liberal approach towards tolerance represents an urgent task confronting those who are concerned about the future of democracy.

Notes

1 Hazard (1973), p. 344.
2 Cited in Mendus (1989), p. 7.
3 Butterfield (1977), p. 573.
4 Walzer (1997), p. xii.
5 Murphy (1997), p. 599.
6 Wolfe (1998), p. 54.
7 See UNESCO (1995).
8 'Introduction' in Heyd (1996), pp. 4 and 5.
9 Horton (1996), p. 37.
10 See UNESCO (1995).
11 Brown (2006), pp. 34–5.
12 Brown (2006), p. 35.
13 Brown (2006), p. 43.
14 Galeotti (2002), p. 5.

15 Association of British Insurers (2010).
16 See Schneier (2009).
17 Galeotti (2002), p. 14.
18 Griffin (2010), p. 27.
19 Balint (2006), p. 4.
20 Ramadan (2010), p. 47.
21 Ramadan (2010), p. 47.
22 See Mendus (1989), p. 77.
23 Ramadan (2010), p. 47.
24 Horton (1996), p. 35.
25 Galeotti (2002), p. 10.
26 Ramadan (2010), p. 48.
27 Brown (2006), p. 189.
28 Brown (2006), p. 187.
29 Brown (2006), p. 6.
30 Brown (2006), p. 7.
31 Brown (2006), pp. 70–1. 'Tolerance emerges at this point as a *supplement* to equality rather than a mere extension of it', variously a 'substitute' or an 'alternative'; ' above all, that which finesses the incompleteness of equality – making equality "true" when it cannot become so on its own terms'.
32 Caldwell (2009).
33 Fitzgerald (1999), p. 13.
34 Apel (1997), pp. 200–1.
35 Galeotti (2002), p. 159.
36 Marcuse (1965), p. 7.

2

Tolerance as a Precious Resource

This chapter explores the historical evolution of the idea of tolerance. The idea of tolerance is always tested by people's pragmatic concerns and agenda, and society does not always prove equal to the task of accepting the demands that tolerance places on it. In the end tolerance turns out to be a precious resource that is in need of constant intellectual renewal.

Over the past half century, Western society has become complacent about the value of tolerance. Numerous books on the subject can barely restrain a sense of contemptuous dismissal. 'Classically, tolerance is a terribly liberal posture, although less "posture" often and more "terrible" than a forthright signalling of distaste, distrust, disapprobation', claims the author of one widely cited introduction to the subject.[1] Such a casual devaluation of what has proved to be an enormously important opening-up of the Western mind is symptomatic of a wider mood of cynicism towards the authority of liberty. Many thinkers have become preoccupied with drawing the boundaries of tolerance and inventing reasons as to why certain opinions and activities should not be tolerated.

Since its inception as a liberal virtue, tolerance has been perceived as a troublesome ideal that requires to be tempered by a constant reality check. One recent contribution argues that 'toleration is not natural' and that it is 'difficult and hard to get used to'; therefore this 'artificial' virtue can only be upheld on pragmatic and prudential grounds.[2] Doubts and questions raised about the virtue of tolerance represent an understandable response to the lack of consistency with which this liberal ideal is practised. The condition of existential uncertainty gives rise to the perception that tolerance of others' beliefs is essential in a world where truth is elusive; and it is precisely the same condition that provokes a disposition towards intolerance. That's one reason why tolerance can never rest on its laurels – its very success serves as an invitation to acts of intolerance.

Kamen rightly notes that tolerance is 'part of the process in history which has led to a gradual development of the principle of human freedom', before adding that this 'development has been by no means regular'.[3] Indeed the experience of history demonstrates that we can never take tolerance for granted. For well over 2,000 years individuals and communities have periodically recognized the necessity, even desirability, of restraining the impulse to repress people's beliefs and interfere in their private affairs. The discovery of tolerance occurred over many centuries. Its elaboration as a powerful ideal was inspired by a variety of calculations, such as the pragmatic concern to avoid violent conflict, the aspiration to develop a sphere of private life immune from political control, the recognition that the road to the truth required the freedom of belief, and the growing appreciation of the significance of moral autonomy. Often it was an expression of the basic aspiration to restrain political power. With the ascendancy of the values of liberty and freedom, tolerance emerged as a virtue associated with the modern imagination in general and with liberalism in particular.

However, it is far easier to uphold tolerance in theory than in practice. Human beings find it difficult to tolerate opinions and practices that they find genuinely objectionable. Hence, as noted in the previous chapter, there is a tendency to apply tolerance selectively. Society's capacity to tolerate is continually tested by new events: as the historian Herbert Butterfield indicates, 'wherever it was established, it became clear that toleration, as a working system, was subject to serious limitations', since its own upholders tended to regard it as only a 'temporary expedient'.[4] The kind of beliefs, opinions and related practices that demand the capacity to tolerate continually change their form and throw up unexpected challenges. The calls for tolerance first emerged in relation to the settling of religious disputes: today, doctrinal differences between Catholics and Protestants rarely test our capacity to be tolerant. Although the question of tolerance is frequently raised in disputes between Westerners and Muslims and between Muslims and Jews, the issue at stake is more national, ethnic and cultural than religious. Indeed by the nineteenth and certainly by the twentieth century it was mainly political and ideological differences and conflicts that tested Western society's capacity for tolerance. Since the 1960s, and especially since the 1980s, the threat of intolerance has mutated into a more cultural and lifestyle form. The so-called culture wars convey an intense mood of moral conflict over issues like sexuality, abortion, identity and health. Today a lack of moral certainty has fostered a climate that is surprisingly uncomfortable with adhering to the value of tolerance – hence we not only have culture wars, but also 'science wars', 'mummy wars' and 'health wars'.

Intolerance is not the only way that people respond to uncertainty. During the seventeenth and eighteenth centuries uncertainty helped to establish the cultural preconditions for the emergence of a tolerant sensibility. One of the principal aims of this book is to explain why societies in the twenty-first century find it so difficult to tolerate uncertainty. To anticipate our argument: it is not uncertainty but the cultural resources through which it is perceived that accounts for the diminishing of a tolerant sensibility.

In previous times intolerance was fuelled by the imperative of upholding faith and duty. It was an article of faith that 'only one form of religion could be true' and that 'anything else must be not merely error, but an actual danger to human soul and to society in general'.[5] In our times it is the lack of faith, otherwise expressed as the difficulty that Western culture has in giving meaning to social experience, which leads to manifestations of intolerance. Consequently, manifestations of intolerance have an arbitrary and unstable character. Bitter disputes over wearing headscarves, eating junk food, promoting scientific research on animals, euthanasia, abortion or global warming have led to the emergence of an unexpected cohort of twenty-first-century heretics. And predictably, calls to ban or censor or criminalize these heretics continually test society's commitment to tolerance. However, the future of society depends on our capacity to stand up for this value, for as Ronald Dworkin reminds us, 'tolerance is the cost we pay for our adventure in liberty'.[6] Tolerance provides us with the intellectual apparatus necessary to navigate the unchartered territory of uncertainty. It involves taking a risk, and having the willingness to embark on a voyage whose destination in unknown.

The long journey

The Ancient Greeks had the first glimmer of the value of toleration. Pericles' famous Funeral Oration eulogizes Athens' culture of freedom: 'freely, we live as citizens, freely both towards that which is commonly shared and towards one another in our daily affairs'. Although Pericles upholds the virtues of public life as the ideal, he recognizes the importance of affording citizens freedom in their private affairs, assuring his audience that 'we are unconstrained in our private business' and 'in our private business we are not suspicious of one another, nor angry with our neighbour if he does what he likes'.[7] Although Pericles' representation of the right of private citizens to be left alone was an idealization of life in ancient Athens, it nevertheless provided a recognition of the need to restrain social interference in the private lives of individuals. In a halting and hesitant manner Pericles' Funeral Oration provides us with a sense of what would, centuries later, be known as tolerance. But this is not quite the same as the seventeenth-century idea of tolerance towards individual belief. As the New Zealand political scientist Richard Mulgan observes, 'in Pericles' speech, nevertheless the tolerance of Athens is justified not in terms of anything due to individuals, but because it has benefited the city as a whole'.[8] To be sure it is the pragmatic concern with the power and social coherence of Athens that provides the justification for tolerance; but the recognition that people who feel that they are free provide a source of strength for the entire community represents in important advance in human thinking about liberty.

The political culture of Athens appeared to be relatively open to the idea of tolerance. Indeed it is possible to interpret Socrates' dialogues as a very early example of harnessing the spirit of tolerance for the pursuit of clarity and truth. Socrates' philosophical method attempts to use the clash of views in an open-ended, tolerant way so that those who are party to the dialogue are free to develop their argument in whatever direction they deem necessary. As far as Socrates was concerned, because we do not know what we think we know, a dialogue with a contrasting viewpoint sensitizes us to the strengths and weaknesses of our arguments and enhances our access to the truth. In this sense Socrates anticipates one of Mill's arguments for tolerance, which is that 'received opinion may be wrong and the heretic right'.[9]

These very early manifestations of the spirit of tolerance in Athens soon became exhausted through setbacks suffered in conflict and war. For centuries to come, even Pericles' very minimalist idea of tolerance was lost. The American historian Donald Kagan has noted that 'in their rational and secular approach, in their commitment to political freedom and individual autonomy in a constitutional, republican and democratic political life, the Athenians of Pericles' day are closer to the values of our era than any culture that has appeared since antiquity'. He added: 'that is why Periclean Athens has such a powerful meaning for us'.[10]

Between Athens in the fifth century BC and seventeenth-century Europe, ideas about tolerance were rarely expressed in a coherent systematic manner. Christianity in its early days questioned the right of the state to force people to accept a certain religion. In the early third century the theologian Tertullian insisted that 'each one is free to adore whom he wants'. He wrote that the 'religion of an individual neither harms nor profits anybody else' and that 'it is against the nature of religion to force religion'.[11] Writing in a similar vein, John Chrysostom, the archbishop of Constantinople, stated that it was not 'right for Christians to eradicate error by constraint and force, but to save humanity by persuasion and reasonableness and gentleness'.[12] Such expressions of tolerance towards what are interpreted as erroneous beliefs are used as evidence by the philosopher J. Budziszewski as proof that 'tolerance is a Christian innovation'.[13] However, this conclusion does not stand up to careful scrutiny. Once Christianity became officially recognized by Roman Emperor Constantine in 313 AD, the church became more and more intolerant. It approved punitive sanctions taken against Arians and Donatists – heterodox Christian sects – by secular authorities. And Saint Augustine's campaign against the Donatists of North Africa in the early fifth century indicated that the persecution of heresy was becoming official policy. Augustine's declaration, 'What death is worse for the soul than the liberty to err', indicated that the church was not prepared to tolerate doctrinal error.[14]

In retrospect this gradual shift in attitude from toleration to the policing of heresy provides an early example of the way in which pragmatic and instrumental calculations influence policies. As long as the Christian church was weak and faced a hostile secular power, its call for freedom to follow its faith was consistent with its aspiration for institutional survival. However, once the church became the official religion and was closely aligned to the state it regarded the tolerance of dissident faiths as a threat to its authority and power. The tendency towards adopting a coercive approach towards those who questioned the official church doctrine was reinforced by the ascendancy of papal political power. By the late twelfth and early thirteenth centuries the leaders of the Church insisted that its authority was greater than that of Kings. In his papal bull *Unam Sanctam* in 1302, Boniface VIII claimed that all authority on earth was vested in the church – two swords ruled the world but 'both swords, the spiritual and the material, are in the power of the Church'.[15]

The expansive theocratic ambition of the church was paralleled by the growth of an increasingly coercive approach towards dissident belief. In such circumstances dissident religious groups adopted the strategy of challenging the 'coercive power of the Church in temporal matters, as the only way to establish toleration for themselves'.[16] In effect they sought to curb the political power of the church, looking to secular rulers for protection and hoping that the feudal nobles would allow them to practise their religious faith. The intertwining of political and religious motives had the effect of ensuring that calls for tolerance were often linked to protest and rebellion against the prevailing order. It was in response to the intolerance of the church that the demand for the right of the individual to dissent and individual conscience gained definition and in outline form came to constitute what would, in the seventeenth century, be characterized as the doctrine of toleration.

Although the Reformation is associated with the rise of the idea of toleration, religious freedom was not a principle upheld by the reformers. In the sixteenth century very few Protestants believed in such a freedom, and their doctrine did not lead directly to the advocacy of religious tolerance. As one historian reminds us, 'if the early Reformers had their way, there would have been no such thing 'as toleration'.[17] Indeed 'almost all' the reformers 'proclaimed an all but unqualified duty of obedience to any and every duly constituted authority'.[18] Reformers typically adopted a selective and pragmatic approach towards religious practices. Luther, who initially demanded toleration, soon swung towards arguing for intolerance towards his religious foes, personifying the schizophrenic attitude towards toleration. Initially, when he was preoccupied with the objective of gaining freedom for his teaching, Luther took a 'firm stand against coercion in matters of religion', attacking the 'compelling of consciences' and the use of state power to 'repress heresy'. In his 1525 writing *The Unfree Will* he declared that 'the conscience must not be bound by anything, except the Word of God'.[19] Not long after publishing this statement Luther became increasingly worried about the threat posed by religiously inspired rebels and heretics. By 1536 Luther fully accepted the suppression of heresy by the state: 'The public authority is bound to repress blasphemy, false doctrine and heresy, and to inflict corporal punishment on those that support such things'.[20]

Luther's inconsistency was shared by most of the early advocates of tolerance. In *Von Weltlicher Uberkeyt* in 1523 he stated that since religious belief was a personal issue, to 'make it a subject of legal prohibitions and penalties is unjust and absurd'.[21] Two years after this statement he called on the secular princes to use force to repress the Anabaptists, and by 1531 'he went over almost completely to the side of those who, for one reason or another, believed in the maintenance of pure religion by force'.[22] During the following century more and more individuals raised objections to the suppression of religious belief. But the tolerance they advocated was invariably qualified and was by no means extended to all forms of religious beliefs. Sebastien Castellion's anti-heresy-hunting manifesto, *De Haereticis, an sint persequendi*, which appeared in 1554 but could not be published until 1612, provided a powerful argument for toleration, with its statement that 'killing a man is not defending a doctrine; it is merely killing a man'.[23] Nevertheless, Castellion insisted that there were limits to tolerance – those who denied the Resurrection and immortality of the soul and 'those who refuse to recognize any human authority may justly be forbidden by the magistrate to teach their doctrines and punished, though not with death, if they persist in doing so'.[24]

Although these early calls for toleration were limited in scope and often motivated by self-interest, they proved to be important for the development of the idea of freedom of belief. Allen noted that the calls for such freedoms by Catholics and Puritans represented an attempt to uphold the 'liberty of their own consciences, not for those of other people', and that it was merely a coincidence in that they 'helped enlarge human freedom'.[25] The rise of the idea of tolerance may have been the unintended consequence of the more restricted objectives raised by the early reformers. But through demanding freedom for themselves they nevertheless contributed to the normalization of an open-minded attitude towards others' beliefs. It is necessary to note that important concepts like freedom and tolerance take centuries to evolve and are as much a consequence of historical accidents and coincidence of events as they are the elaboration of new ideas.

By the late sixteenth century some very powerful arguments supporting religious freedoms could be heard. In 1565, the Italian-born theologian Jacobus Acontius argued for the absolute freedom of religion. 'The search for truth must begin with doubt and the road to truth lies through free discussion and inquiry', he stated, followed by the conclusion that 'if freedom be established truth will be found and prevail'.[26] With Jacobus Acontius the idea of religious freedom became linked to the pursuit of the truth. In the course of the decades that followed, European society became gradually more and more hospitable to the flourishing of this powerful liberal idea.

One important reason for the growing influence of the idea of toleration was the crisis of belief experienced by European societies in the seventeenth century. Trevor-Roper's seminal essay 'The general crisis of the seventeenth century' discusses the powerful sense of crisis that prevailed, concluding that: 'To contemporary observers it seemed that society itself was in crisis, and that this crisis was general in Europe'.[27] The crisis of the seventeenth century called the old certainties into question. In such circumstances many thinkers could no longer accept traditional truths as self-evident. 'What men craved to know was what they were to believe, and what they were not to believe', writes Hazard.[28] What Hazard describes as a 'crisis of historical consciousness' expressed the growth of doubt and uncertainty towards the meaning of the past and the relevance of traditional values. The French philosopher Pierre Bayle (1647–1706), an advocate of toleration towards different religious beliefs, argued for this principle on the grounds that human beings lacked certain knowledge about the will of God. The world lacked the certainty afforded by the unquestioned acceptance of tradition and Bayle feared that much of what had been accepted as the truth would prove to be false. He argued: 'I have said it before, and I say it again; it is the purest delusion to suppose that because an idea has been handed down from time immemorial to succeeding generations, it may not be entirely false'.[29]

Bayle's doubt about the status of tradition was also linked to his embrace of reason as an instrument for the pursuit of the truth. His belief that 'no mystery is insolvable by human reason' summed up the belief upheld by an influential minority of European thinkers. The growing tendency to question the traditional version of the past meant that the very authority of historical knowledge became the subject of controversy. Instead of serving as a guide to action, history was increasingly perceived as an unreliable record of the past. *Uncertainty in History*, the title of the 1668 book by the French sceptic François de La Mothe Le Vayer (1558–1672), expressed the attitude of a new school of historical criticism. A sense of estrangement from the past even led to questions being raised about the status and authority of the Bible. Sceptics accused historians of bias, and claims that texts were based on forged sources were rife. It was in the late sixteenth century that the word 'critical' became fashionable and in 1700 one scholar characterized his era as the 'age of criticism'.[30] Arguably, it was the French philosopher Montaigne (1533–92) who most systematically called into question the pre-existing Renaissance knowledge of the past, and helped 'reduce the authority of antiquity as a collection of moral and epistemological exemplars'.[31]

There were many reasons for the crisis of historical consciousness in the seventeenth century. Overseas travel confronted the European imagination with the realization that there existed numerous systems of beliefs and customs that guided people's behaviour; and the recognition that different cultures sought answers through practising different customs called into question the belief that there was only one way of organizing society. In these circumstances of existential doubt, science and the use of reason appeared as an effective alternative to relying on dogma and faith. Humanist thinkers such as Erasmus (1466–1536) and sceptical philosophers like Montaigne rejected the doctrines of the church and upheld the autonomy of human reason.

The weakening of belief in tradition and the dogma of the church was at least in part reinforced by the outbreak of religious conflict and doctrinal disputes. During the sixteenth century, the challenge to the authority of the Roman Catholic Church led to the proliferation of religious sects and theological doctrines. These disputes became increasingly bitter, leading in the seventeenth century to war and conflict. Bloody disputes like the Thirty Years War, the violent conflict between Protestant Huguenots and Catholics in France, and the tension between religiously motivated parties during the English Civil War (1642–60), gradually convinced the European elites that religious intolerance had to be managed and curbed. In the case of England, the experience of destructive conflict over doctrinal differences 'led to a shift in the thinking of educated elites on the relationship between religion and society'.[32] The realization that religious differences and disputes had become a fact of life led a significant section of the political elite to adopt an increasingly tolerant attitude towards them.

Pragmatic concerns dictated the first halting steps towards toleration. In late sixteenth-century France, the Huguenots sought to secure their way of life through gaining a degree of official toleration. They assumed that gaining such a concession was realistic because an 'influential group of moderate Catholics had by that time come to the conclusion that any attempt to impose a policy of religious uniformity by force would constitute a serious tactical even if not a moral mistake'.[33] The willingness to accept the right of former religious foes to practise their beliefs was part of the platform of a group of Catholic elites called *les politiques*, who argued that 'uniformity was no longer worth preserving, however valuable it might be itself, if the cost of enforcing it seemed liable to be the destruction of the commonwealth'.[34] With the survival of the integrity of France at stake, a limited form of religious toleration was seen as an acceptable price to pay. In 1598 the Edict of Nantes granted Protestants full civil rights and the right to worship openly – albeit in specified regions. Although this Edict was revoked in 1685, leading to the flight of the Huguenots from France, it was evident that there could be no return to the intolerant regime of the old Inquisition.

There is little doubt that the recognition that the religious enemy could not be crushed without suffering unacceptable losses encouraged *les politiques* and others to opt for a compromise formula. Butterfield believes that from this standpoint, toleration 'was not so much an ideal, a positive end, that people wanted to establish for its own sake' but a 'retreat to the next best thing, a last resort for those who often still hated one another, but found it impossible to go on fighting any more'.[35] But the recognition that religious coercion threatened to undermine, if not destroy, the body politic coincided with a growing appreciation of the difficulty of gaining access to religious truth. With the discrediting of the capacity to possess infallible knowledge of the Divine Will, the practice of hunting down and persecuting heretics lost its legitimacy. Concern with the capacity of humans to gain access to the truth fostered a climate where epistemological toleration could thrive.

Epistemological toleration is underpinned by the conviction that opinions and beliefs should be tolerated because it is either impossible to force people to give up their beliefs or because it is wrong to prevent people from finding their way to the truth. Such sentiments were forcefully advocated by Milton, Spinoza and especially by Locke. Spinoza (1632–77) understood the problem of intolerance from his personal experience. This Jewish philosopher was denounced as a heretic for his denial of revelation and cast out of the synagogue. His *Theological-Political Treatise* (1670) provided an important argument for the freedom of belief, in that the state need not attempt to control or regulate people's belief and should confine itself to managing their action. Nine years later John Locke (1632–1704) wrote what would prove to be the single most important statement on religious toleration. His *Letter Concerning Toleration* (1689) can be interpreted as one of the founding documents of what would become modern liberalism.

During the past century Locke has been often criticized for confining his argument to the advocacy of religious toleration. It should be recalled that his was an era where religious persecution was rife and where the involvement of the state in doctrinal disputes threatened to unravel the body politic. In such circumstances upholding religious liberty represented an important step in a long journey that would eventually lead to the expansion of freedom and democracy. Like Spinoza, Locke attempted to put the case for toleration by 'separating the realm of religious belief from the realm of religious practice – separating individuals' religious beliefs from their social actions, including their religious actions'.[36] The distinction that Spinoza and Locke drew between belief and action served as a point of departure for the elaboration of the two distinct spheres of the private and the public: a conceptual distinction that would prove indispensable for the subsequent evolution of liberal theories.

Locke argued that religious beliefs, which are held in people's heads or hearts, are not appropriate targets for state control. His principle argument was 'the claim that religious belief cannot be secured by the coercive means characteristic of state action'.[37] In effect Locke argued that the attempt by governments to suppress dissident religious belief was likely to be futile, and unlikely to achieve a change in people's beliefs. It would simply lead to the outward display of conformity and fail to cultivate genuine belief.

Locke took the view that the coercive indoctrination of belief by the state does not lead to genuine conviction, and the very attempt to pursue such policy calls into question the rationality of political authority. His call for the toleration of a diversity of religious belief was also influenced by the belief that truth cannot be imposed from without: this requires an internal quest for answers. The internal realm of belief, rather than the external jurisdiction of action, constitutes the focus for Locke's argument for toleration. Locke argues that religious practice, like all forms of action, must be subject to the laws of society, but he insists that religious rituals and practices must not be curbed by government for religious reasons. As an illustration of this point, he refers to the case of animal sacrifice, stating that government ought not curb this practice on religious grounds, but that it can prevent it if its decision is informed by secular rather than religious motives. In an often-cited passage, Locke writes that the 'slaughter of beasts' could be banned if the state decided that 'increasing the stock of cattle' had become essential for the welfare of its agriculture. However, in that case 'the law is not made about a religious but a political matter; nor is the sacrifice, but the slaughter of calves thereby prohibited'.[38]

From Locke's perspective a secular society ought not to prevent a mosque from using a loudspeaker to call the faithful to prayer, or a church from ringing its bells, on religious grounds. It could, however, bar religious institutions from performing such acts if they violated laws linked to noise pollution. Of course Locke recognized that governments could use ostensibly secular arguments for justifying religious discrimination and intolerance, and insisted that a ruler 'ought to be very careful' not to 'misuse his authority to the oppression of any church under pretence of public good'.[39] As Mendus states, Locke does not think 'there is a right to freedom of worship as such, but only a right not to have one's worship interfered with for religious ends'.[40] Nevertheless, Locke made an enormous contribution by establishing religious belief as a domain of social experience that required protection from state. Although he did not elaborate a comprehensive theory of liberty, his argument about belief would provide the foundation for a more enlightened attitude towards freedom of belief and of speech in general.

Locke's attempt to reconcile the protection of religious freedom with the right of the state to regulate people's action represented a major step in the development of the liberal idea of tolerance. As Mendus writes, 'Locke's case is thus a minimalist and pragmatic case against persecution.'[41] His pragmatism also informed the careful manner with which he sought to establish a balance between protecting individuals from religious persecution with the defence of the secular political order. Locke refused to extend the principle of toleration to Catholics and atheists: accordingly, he too can be accused of adopting a selective approach towards tolerance. However, Locke's non-toleration of Catholics and atheists is consistent with his argument, and was justified on the grounds of political expediency rather than as a matter of religious necessity: these groups were not to be discriminated against on religious grounds but on political ones. Locke regarded them as a threat to government: Catholicism would not be protected because it allegedly owned allegiance to a foreign power, and atheists would be denied toleration because they owned loyalty to no one.

Whatever the limits of Locke's contribution, through his argument for a separate jurisdiction of belief that requires protection from the actions of the state he helped sensitize future writers to the need for affirming a clear distinction between private and public life. As it has evolved, the liberal ideal of toleration, which presupposes a distinction between private and public life, accords great significance to the protection of personal – not just religious – belief. Since Locke's time the significance attached to private belief has expanded to encompass other personal freedoms because it is recognized that it is through being able to develop and pursue one's individual thought that we can gain a glimmer of the truth.

During the two centuries that followed the publication of the *Letter Concerning Toleration*, Locke's idea of tolerance represented the liberal statement on the subject. However, in the nineteenth century J. S. Mill deepened the idea of tolerance by explicitly linking it to the pursuit of truth. For Mill, the road to truth is the road to toleration. He eloquently outlined an argument that posited the freedom of belief and speech as the precondition for the discovery of the truth. His important insight has as its premise the affirmation and respect for the individual's moral agency and autonomy. Although Mill presented tolerance as essential for the discovery of the truth, his case for 'the toleration of opinion is not merely the concern for the correctness of conclusions, but for the whole spiritual, moral, and intellectual health of the inner life'.[42]

As noted in Chapter 6, the grounding of tolerance in the exercise of autonomy lends this idea a powerful moral dimension. Through extending tolerance from the liberty of belief to the freedom to exercise autonomy, it acquired depth and meaning for personal experience. Mill's argument that an individual's 'own mode of laying out his existence is best, not because it is the best in itself, but because it is his own mode' provides a powerful statement about the fundamental moral status of individual freedom and choice. 'In saying this, Mill implies that there is a truth about the best way to lead one's life, but that it is better that people should find their own way to the truth than that truth be imposed', notes Mendus.[43]

Embracing uncertainty

The liberal idea of tolerance was born in an era of exceptional uncertainty. In the seventeenth century uncertainty and doubt became a dominant cultural force that influenced the way society confronted the existential questions it faced. As Brendan Dooley's history of the period observes, many of the truths that explained the way that the world worked came under attack, as well as the fundamental tenets of religion and philosophy.

In such circumstances 'speculation eroded the foundations of many examined truths' and its effects were compounded and heightened by 'quite independent and specifically directed doubt about what people were told in the political realm'.[44] Dooley's study of the ascendancy of doubt is focused on the emergence of new forms of writing and journalism which turned 'writers into speculators, information into opinion, and readers into critics'. This was a development not unlike the rise of digitally driven media in the late twentieth century but with a far more profound consequence for the contestation of cultural authority. One outcome was the emergence of a culture of scepticism that engulfed intellectual and political life. As Dooley stated, 'whatever other forms of disbelief the century may have offered, the historical scepticism of the late seventeenth century threatened the very bonds of trust upon which early modern government was based, provoking a response at the level of practice as well as of theory'.[45] In such circumstances, religious belief itself was challenged and gradually the power of dogma over society diminished in strength.

The information revolution of the seventeenth century and its corrosive impact on traditional truths both expressed and reinforced the climate of uncertainty that characterized this era. The experience of history indicates that the absence of certainty creates disorientation and confusion, as well as a demand for knowledge and answers. In the unique setting of the seventeenth century the sudden disintegration of the truths that had motivated people for many generations produced an intellectual crisis that called into question the very capacity to know. The rise of philosophical scepticism expressed the conviction that the truth cannot be known and in some cases it led to the denial of its very existence. In such a cultural climate even those who did not embrace an explicitly sceptical outlook were often shaken in their beliefs, and the recognition of human fallibility in the attainment of truths became prevalent.

Uncertainty as a condition of life provides a compelling sociological motif for the valuation of tolerance. It is precisely because we cannot be certain of truth that we must allow for the greater openness to other people's beliefs and opinions. In such circumstances there existed a clear epistemological justification for toleration: uncertainty demands that people should be free to express and pursue their quest for the truth. As Mill argued in a different historical context, 'if any opinion is compelled to silence, that opinion may, for aught we certainly know be true' and he warned that 'to deny this is to assume our own infallibility'.[46] From this perspective the state of uncertainty about the truth demands a tolerant orientation towards the opinion of others.

In the seventeenth century, doctrinal anxieties often led to a sceptical justification for toleration. And indeed Locke's own approach was influenced by the crisis of belief. But it is much more useful to perceive the practice of tolerance as an attempt to find the road to truth in the context of moral uncertainty. As Robin Barrow contends in his introduction to moral philosophy, tolerance is a 'key virtue because of the limited nature of our legitimate moral certainty'. Moral uncertainty does not mean that society lacks moral knowledge or has no idea about truth, but that there are important questions whose answer eludes us, meaning that we should be open to the possibility that those who disagree with us may possess insights that can contribute to the process of moral clarification. Our difficulty in being certain about truth does not mean that we cannot comprehend it or that there is no such thing as the truth. Moral uncertainty merely imposes an obligation to be open-minded and tolerant towards the views and behaviour of others. Barrow argues that toleration must be integral to any 'genuine moral theory' since it is 'necessary in proportion to the degree of our legitimate and unavoidable uncertainty'. To illustrate this point, Barrow refers to the current controversy about euthanasia: 'If we cannot be sure whether euthanasia is acceptable or not, then clearly it cannot be right either to prohibit or to prescribe it: we must, on moral grounds, learn to live with the uncertainty and divergence of opinion'.[47]

With the benefit of hindsight, the ideas about toleration thrown up in the seventeenth century can be seen as one of European society's cultural and intellectual responses to the prevailing climate of uncertainty. This response attempted to combine a commitment to the discovery of truth with affording people the freedom to find their own path to it. Not everyone shared the open-minded attitude that linked the freedom of belief to the pursuit of truth. Many responded to this crisis of historical consciousness by giving up on the possibility of knowing the truth, while others tried to close down discussion and demanded that the truths of the past should not be questioned. Both of these responses reflect a profound sense of anxiety regarding the uncertain status of moral knowledge. Yet uncertainty need not be perceived as a problem: it can be seen as an opportunity for gaining greater certainty through the development of knowledge. An open and tolerant cultural orientation can creatively harness our uncertainties to the development of humanity's moral and intellectual understanding.

Unfortunately, human society often finds it difficult to have an open-minded engagement with uncertainty. In the seventeenth century – and in the current era – one response to uncertainty was to abolish it through policing belief and closing down debate. Those who are uncomfortable with embracing uncertainty are likely to be drawn towards intolerance, which is why many seventeenth-century European societies were torn between opting for tolerance and hunting down heretics.

Witch-hunting: the response of intolerance to uncertainty

In the seventeenth century, many of the values and attributes associated with modern society were forged. This was an era that saw the gradual ascendancy of science and rationality, and as we noted above, a growing acceptance of toleration and freedom. But as Trevor-Roper reminds us, the 'Scientific Revolution was not free of superstition'. The opening of the European mind was paralleled by the rise of insecure but strident voices who sought refuge in dogma and superstition; Trevor-Roper writes that 'beneath the surface of an ever more sophisticated society' lurked 'dark passions and inflammable credulities' including anxieties and obsessions about witchcraft.[48] Witch-hunting acquired momentum in the sixteenth century and became increasingly powerful in the first half of the seventeenth century. Trevor-Roper argues that the anti-witch hysteria only began to subside after the 1650s, gradually exhausting itself in the following decades.

One of the most disturbing puzzles posed by historians is how to account for the active role played by many of the outstanding intellectuals and scientific thinkers in the promotion of the sixteenth- and seventeenth-century witch-hunts. It is widely known that some of the leading thinkers of this era actively advocated the hunting down and torturing of witches. Numerous questions have been raised about why Jean Bodin (1530–96), France's pre-eminent thinker and leading rationalist, also published a major text advocating a vigorous crusade against the practice of witchcraft. Bodin did not just acquiesce to the witchcraft scare: he played an active role in the promoting of this fear. He 'roared terribly at mild judges' who were reluctant to burn witches and accused them of 'abetting witchcraft and even of being witches themselves'.[49] Bodin's intolerance towards those who held sceptical views about his crusade acquired an ominous tone, with his call to punish with the utmost rigour the witches and 'strike awe into some by the punishment of others'.[50]

Trevor-Roper describes Bodin as the 'Aristotle, the Montesquieu of the sixteenth century, the prophet of comparative history' and 'who yet, in 1580 wrote the book which, more than any other, reanimated the witch-fires throughout Europe'. He remarks that reading Bodin 'demanding death at the stake not only for witches, but for all those who do not believe every grotesque detail of the new demonology, is a sobering experience'.[51]

One study of seventeenth-century French Catholic demonologists describes them as 'sincere defenders of religious orthodoxy as they understood it'.[52] Although history may judge them as bigoted zealots who were responsible for fuelling violent episodes of panic, they perceived themselves as 'participants in a violent age of disorder, an age of combat between the forces of light and the forces of darkness'.[53] As far as they were concerned they were protecting society from subversive satanic influences and deeds. Unable to engage with the confusions thrown up in such uncertain times, they believed that the devil's hand was everywhere sowing mistrust and confusion. The demonologists believed that they were providing a public service in correcting the serious theological errors of the peers and raising the awareness of an otherwise complacent and tolerant public.

The demonologists of the seventeenth century were bit-
terly hostile to the idea of toleration and attacked those who
doubted their cause. In their eyes scepticism constituted a form
of heresy. 'Many people have held that there are no demons and
that it is foolish to dispute and even more to believe the evil
deeds attributed to them and to their supporters', complained
Pierre de Lancre, a demonologist judge from Bordeaux.[54] For
de Lancre and his colleagues the scepticism among the educated classes was a serious problem that had to be overcome
in order to deal with the threat. The targets of the demonologist theologians were 'atheists', 'sceptics' and 'libertines'.[55] The
argument that scepticism towards witchcraft was the first step
to atheism was also pursued by pro-witchcraft pamphleteers in
England.[56] In his influential text, Jean Bodin asserted that those
who are sceptical about the reality of witchcraft are usually
witches themselves. Witch-hunters were also critical of judicial
incredulity, and frequently denounced magistrates for being
soft on witchcraft. According to one study, these demonologists attempted to hold the line against the uncertainties and
confusions sown by representatives of the new culture of doubt.
Jonathan Pearl writes that 'the authors of demonological tracts
were not simply zealous propagators of old traditions or cynical oppressors of free-thought and popular peasant culture':
they 'developed the science of demons as sincere embattled
defenders of faith'.[57]

Belief in witchcraft was not confined to intellectuals who
were concerned with the rise of rationalism and scepticism.
Many early modern adherents of scientific thinking believed
in the existence of witches. The title page of Joseph Glanvill's
1666 booklet *A Philosophical Endeavour towards the Defence
of the being of Witches and Apparitions* announced that it
was written by a 'Member of the Royal Society'. Glanvill was

an enthusiastic defender of the 'new science', and vigorously defended the Royal Society in his writings. Nevertheless, this upholder of rationalistic principles also felt compelled to write a robust defence of a medieval superstition.[58] It is important to note that many of his contemporaries in the scientific world shared his sentiments: Sir Francis Bacon, Sir Thomas Browne, Henry More and Robert Boyle appeared to accept the existence of witchcraft. It has been suggested that the 'only English thinker of first-rate importance during the seventeenth century who unmistakably and emphatically opposed the belief in witches was Thomas Hobbes'.[59]

In the current era, the witch-hunting craze of the seventeenth century would be interpreted as a form of moral panic. That such an extreme and ferocious response was adopted by otherwise intelligent and responsible public figures can only be explained by the existential anxieties provoked by their fears around uncertainty. That they opted for demonology to give meaning to their predicament revealed their mistrust of people's capacity for moral autonomy and their potential to do what was right for their community. This apprehension towards the right of individuals to pursue the truth was clearly formulated by Bossuet:

> And so we get a clear idea of the real fundamental meaning of the words Catholic and Heretic. A heretic is one who has his own opinion. What does having an opinion mean? It means following one's own ideas, one's own particular notions. Whereas the Catholic, on the other hand, is what the name signifies, that is to say one who, not relying on his own private judgment, puts his trust in the Church, and defers to her teaching.[60]

Bossuet's unambiguous equation of heresy with the 'following one's own ideas' clearly expresses the counterargument to the toleration of belief. Although it represents a futile attempt to restore certainty in an otherwise troubled era, this response continues to animate a significant section of society to this day. The counterpoint to Bossuet's stigmatization of individual belief is provided by Mill's criticism and challenge to custom and conformity. Indeed his famous essay *On Liberty* (1859) can be interpreted as a celebration of the heretic. Mill did not simply advocate tolerance and freedom of thought as a method for discovering the truth, but also, as Villa notes, as a 'means for dissolving misplaced certainty'.[61] Mill perceived the heretic as someone who at worst forced society to account for its opinions but who at best could point to truths that eluded others. Mill's argument for tolerance is in part based on the insight that when opinion becomes unquestioned and too secure, it loses its capacity to capture truth. That is why he took the view that 'even if received opinion is true, heretical opinions are necessary to retain "lively apprehension" of their truth' and insisted that 'moral complacency leads us to falsify or drain the substance from their most valuable part of conventional opinion'.[62]

It is the insight gained through questioning and the clash of ideas that provides society with the intellectual security needed to engage with insecurity. Without the capacity to question even the beliefs that we hold to be true society risks making them false. That is why even the most cherished beliefs or the most advanced scientific opinion can only benefit from the criticism mounted by the heretic and sceptic. Today, as in the past, Bossuet and Mill offer us the alternative approach to dealing with uncertainty.

Conclusion

As the experience of the past indicates, there are numerous arguments for dealing with uncertainty. One of the most compelling justifications for toleration in a modern society is that we are confronted intellectually and morally with uncertainty. In such circumstances adopting an open mind towards the views of others is not simply a matter of polite behaviour but an epistemological and a moral necessity. Adopting an open mind should not be equated with not taking ideas seriously, or being indifferent to people's beliefs. It represents a commitment to the pursuit of knowledge through a dialogue. It also takes the view that truth cannot be simply handed down and absorbed, but is discovered through a clash of competing views.

Since the seventeenth century tolerance has often been confused with a reluctance to take truth seriously. From time to time philosophers and other intellectuals have responded to uncertainty by adopting the view that humanity has no certain way of knowing that it knows. In some cases scepticism about the capacity to know and discover the truth has led to a form of toleration that disassociates it from the pursuit of truth. In the sixteenth and seventeenth centuries the sceptical justification for tolerance represented a major advance over the prevailing regime of intolerance. However, its disavowal of the potential for discovering truths divested freedom of belief of its important moral dimension. In more recent times the positive and critical edge of a sceptical epistemology has been lost. What remains is a relativistic epistemology that mistakes tolerance for indifference and a refusal to judge. This approach represents acquiescence to uncertainty, and ends up enthroning its refusal to take truth seriously.

Whereas relativism seeks to celebrate uncertainty, intolerance seeks to abolish it. Despite the powerful legacy of liberal tolerance, Western societies often adopt intolerant practices to deal with our uncertain times. Contemporary public life is afflicted by a self-serving and selective orientation towards freedom. Intolerance comes in many guises and often the apparently multiculturalist relativist turns out to be no less intolerant than a self-conscious proponent of religious dogma. That so many different groups, political organizations and cultural elites have lost sight of the importance of tolerance should alert us to the importance of restating and developing the case for this precious resource for handling uncertainty.

Notes

1 King (1976), p. 11.
2 Sabl (2009), p. 512.
3 Kamen (1967), p. 7.
4 Butterfield (1977), p. 578.
5 Butterfield (1977), p. 575.
6 Dworkin (1993), p. 167.
7 See 'Pericles' funeral oration', in Thucydides, *Peloponnesian War*, ii. 34–46. Available at: www.englishare.net/literature/ POL-HS-Pericles.htm (accessed 17 February 2011).
8 Mulgan (1984), p. 13.
9 See Villa (2001), p. 98.
10 Kagan (1991), p. 10.
11 Cited in Kamen (1967), p. 8.
12 Cited in Budziszewski (1992), p. 291. John Chrysostom lived *c.* 347–407.
13 Budziszewski (1992), p. 289.
14 Cited in Kamen (1967), p. 14.
15 Cited in Kamen (1967), p. 15.
16 Kamen (1967), p. 17.
17 Allen (1964), p. 3.
18 Allen (1964), p. 8.
19 Cited in Kamen (1967), p. 30.

20 Cited in Kamen (1967), p. 20.
21 Cited in Allen (1964), p. 25.
22 Allen (1964), p. 25.
23 Allen (1964), p. 93.
24 Cited in Allen (1964), p. 93.
25 Allen (1964), p. 209.
26 Cited in Allen (1964), p. 100.
27 Trevor-Roper (1959), p. 31.
28 Hazard (1973), p. 8.
29 Cited in Hazard (1973), p. 188.
30 Burke (1998).
31 Sedley (1998), p. 1082.
32 Zaret (1989), p. 172.
33 See Skinner (1984), p. 249.
34 Skinner (1984), p. 250.
35 Butterfield (1977), p. 573.
36 Beattie (2004), p. 372.
37 Waldron (1988), p. 67.
38 Locke (1983), p. 42.
39 Locke (1983), p. 40.
40 Mendus (1989), p. 37.
41 Mendus (1989), p. 34.
42 Edwards (1988), p. 107.
43 Mendus (1989), p. 77.
44 Dooley (1999), p. 2.
45 Dooley (1999), p. 2.
46 Mill (2008).
47 Barrow (2007), pp. 99 and 9.
48 Trevor-Roper (2001), pp. 11–12.
49 Cited in Heinsohn and Steiger (1999), pp. 436–7.
50 Heinsohn and Steiger (1999), p. 442.
51 Trevor-Roper (1969), p. 47.
52 Pearl (1983), p. 457.
53 Pearl (1983), p. 458.
54 Pearl (1983), p. 458.
55 Pearl (1983), pp. 461–2.
56 See Prior (1932), p. 178.

57 See Pearl (1983), p. 467.
58 See Prior (1932), p. 178.
59 Prior (1932), p. 170.
60 Cited in Hazard (1973), p. 233.
61 Villa (2001), p. 74.
62 Villa (2001), p. 98.

3

The Fossilization of Identity

The aim of this chapter is to contest the current tendency to redefine tolerance as a concept that informs attitudes towards group and cultural identities. Used in this way, tolerance ceases to possess any epistemological significance or moral virtue; rather, through its perfunctory validation of identity the concept becomes complicit in closing down discussion.

As has been emphasized, the act of tolerance should not be confused with a gesture of polite behaviour. Although the idea of toleration evolved as a response to religious strife, it is more than a pragmatic method for managing conflicts of beliefs. One important argument for tolerance is the importance of restraining political power so that the freedom of belief and opinion can be pursued. Another reason why tolerance is vitally significant is because of its potential for tempering the negative consequences of uncertainty through creating the conditions for gaining greater clarity. This is accomplished through the process of debate among competing views and opinions: from this perspective, even views that are deemed to be false can serve the positive end of forcing others to develop and clarify their opinions. The tolerance of dissent and of opinions that are regarded as erroneous or offensive is motivated by the conviction that it is only when no belief is beyond question that insight into truth can be gained.

According to Mill even the most authoritative doctrines of his time, such as Newtonian philosophy, required exposure to interrogation if it was to communicate truths. Mill took the view that only through questioning could we ensure that we neglect nothing 'that could give the truth a chance to reach us' and hope that 'if there is a better truth' it will eventually reach us. He added that this is the 'sole amount of certainty attainable by a fallible being', and tolerance is the only way attaining it.[1]

The justification for toleration is not merely epistemological. Truth-seeking and tolerance have an important moral dimension. As Edwards notes, whatever the costs of tolerance in terms of putting up with obnoxious views, Mill insists that the 'duty of toleration should be held as an ethical conviction'.[2] The freedom of belief is linked to the freedom to exercise individual judgement, to challenge other people's ideas and to test out one's own. It is only through the exercise of individual judgement that belief is internalized and ceases to be unreflected received opinion. From this perspective, even truths can turn into superstitious dogma if they are merely held on faith: indeed, without the exercise of individual judgement, the meaning and intellectual content of an opinion becomes exhausted and transformed into prejudice. That is why, as Edwards argues, 'Mill's case for the toleration of opinion is not merely a concern for the correctness of conclusions, but for the whole spiritual, moral, and intellectual health of the inner life'.[3] It is when individuals arrive at views and beliefs through their own effort and experience that they become part of a wider human adventure of finding new truths. This occurs through different individuals exercising their judgement through interacting and contributing to the development of humanity's intellectual legacy.

Unfortunately, society finds it difficult to be genuinely and consistently open to criticism and dissent. This is no less a feature of the contemporary era of uncertainty. In the early twenty-first-century era the contestation of ideas lacks robust cultural support, and the rhetoric of public engagement notwithstanding, there is considerable reluctance to respond to the challenge posed by uncertainty by embracing the open-ended pursuit of ideas. How a society responds to uncertainty is influenced by the support that its culture is able to provide to intellectual and scientific experimentation and to the pursuit of knowledge. In contemporary times society is ambivalent about its attitude towards knowledge. It is even claimed that we inhabit a world of 'unknown unknowns' where certainty is an elusive commodity.[4] Consequently, the healthy scepticism of the early modern era has ossified into a cynical disavowal of seeking truths.[5]

Twenty-first-century intellectual currents often dismiss the project of pursuing the truth as an outdated and discredited legacy of the Enlightenment. Consequently, many Western democratic societies find it difficult genuinely to value serious controversy and debate, and differences of views often lead to calls to close down discussion. This intolerance of sceptical opinion is striking in relation to the debate on climate change: for example, in the way in which Ed Miliband, in his former capacity as the UK's Secretary of State for Energy and Climate Change, declared war on dissident voices: 'There are a whole variety of people who are sceptical, but who they are is less important than what they are saying, and what they are saying is profoundly dangerous'.[6] Ed Miliband's brother, David, in his former capacity as the UK's Secretary of State for the Environment, echoed this censorious sentiment: 'The debate over the science of climate change is well and truly over'. The assertion that the uncertainty associated with climate change is best resolved through closing down debate is illustrative of the ease with which policymakers and opinion formers can demand the silencing of 'dangerous' ideas.

Cynicism about the value of debate in clarifying ideas is evident in relation to the way that the exercise of individual judgement and autonomy is considered. There is a discernable tendency to interpret an individual's intelligence, attitude and disposition, not so much as an outcome of self-reflection, education or intellectual development, but as the result of a variety of innate characteristics. In education, the fashionable theory of 'multiple intelligences' is based on the fatalistic assumption that children possess a pre-programmed blend of different intelligences that dispose them to learn in different ways.[7] Even people's beliefs and opinions are represented as expressions of their genetic dispositions: so research by scientists from the universities of California and Harvard claim to have discovered a 'liberal gene' that opens people to new ideas and alternative lifestyles. From this perspective, liberalism, tolerance and a disposition to new ideas is less something that is acquired through the exercise of individual judgement than it is a consequence of a 'transmitter' in the brain called DRD4.[8] Moral reasoning itself is depicted as a function that can be explained through the workings of the brain; the philosopher Paul Thagard has offered an explanation of the meaning of life through drawing on research from neuroscience rather than on moral and culturally informed beliefs.[9]

In the contemporary era the question of tolerance is rarely linked to the challenge of managing and judging conflicting beliefs. Our times are characterized not only by the exhaustion of ideologies but also by a relative loss of faith in the power of ideas. The religious conflicts of the seventeenth and eighteenth centuries, and the ideological battles of the nineteenth and much of the twentieth centuries, have given way to clashes of identities, lifestyles and cultures. These are not so much disputes about beliefs and opinions as existential conflicts about who one is. One response to these disputes has been to redeploy the idea of tolerance to deal with what are, in fact, group conflicts. Current calls for tolerance evoke the threat of uncontained ethnic, racial or cultural conflicts and offer tolerance as the only responsible response to such threats. The focus is on tolerating people for who they are rather than for their views and behaviour.

Consequently, tolerance is rarely justified on the ground that it is a prerequisite for intellectual clarification and gaining insights into the truth; and nor is it linked to the exercise of an individual's moral autonomy. Moreover, the interpretation of tolerance as an attitude towards groups assumes that it is dealing with a homogeneous entity. The fossilization of identity conveyed through the assumption of the homogeneity of a group's individual members is the very antithesis of the premise of autonomy.

When tolerance is redefined to encompass group relations its very meaning alters. Tolerance is not simply expanded from the individual to wider groups; the concept becomes transformed from a concept directed towards opening the mind to competing beliefs and opinions to a concept that affirms different clusters of people for who they are, and in turn leads to the censoring of discussion.

The meaning of the shift from individual to group

The reinterpretation of tolerance as a concept directed towards the management of group rights is often self-consciously acknowledged by its proponents. Michael Walzer recognizes that 'individual rights may well lie at the root of every sort of toleration', but shifts the focus towards groups, insisting that he is interested in the tolerance of 'those rights primarily when they are exercised in common . . . or when they are claimed by groups on behalf of their members'.[10] Walzer writes: 'My subject is toleration – or, perhaps better, the peaceful coexistence of groups of people with different histories, cultures, and identities, which is what toleration makes possible'.[11]

Those who uphold the interpretation of toleration as the management of relationships between groups base their arguments on the conviction that we live in a world of endemic inter-group tension and conflict, whose destructive outcomes need to be carefully managed. 'The difficulty with toleration is that it seems to be once necessary and impossible', states one writer on this subject, adding that 'it is necessary where different groups have conflicting beliefs – moral, political, or religious – and realize that there is no alternative to their living together, that is to say, no alternative except armed conflict'.[12] From this perspective what makes toleration 'necessary' may well make its realization 'impossible', since legal instruments may not be adequate to contain the passions that fuel such conflicts.

The reinterpretation of tolerance to connote an attitude towards different people and groups has gained force during the second half of the twentieth century. Although toleration was continually subject to sloppy usage, as with any widely employed concept, it was in the aftermath of the Nazi experience that it began to acquire its current meaning as that of an open-minded attitude towards other ethnic, cultural and religious groups. In the United States the term toleration was adopted to deal with the problems posed by a multi-ethnic society. In this context, toleration was often used to signal a positive attitude towards an America that flourished through accepting the contribution and way of life of its different immigrant communities. Consequently, this word was often deployed as a companion to the term 'pluralism'. As the American political philosopher Robert Paul Wolff argued in the 1960s, in his country pluralism involved not so much the acceptance of individual beliefs and behaviour as the 'celebration of primary group diversity'.[13] Throughout the post–Second World War era this pluralistic model of toleration was transformed into a culturally upheld and prescribed etiquette towards minorities.

In a world where the destructive consequences of racist nationalism and violence were all too evident, the protection of minorities and of disparaged groups became a central concern of democratically inspired policymakers and intellectuals. It was in such circumstances that terms like 'racial tolerance' and 'tolerance towards Jews' acquired widespread usage. Imperceptibly, the meaning of toleration shifted from protecting people's beliefs from state coercion to that of group affirmation. This rhetorical shift towards the toleration of racial and religious minorities has been extended to embrace the numerous identities and lifestyles that have evolved in the post-1960s era. Tolerance is often promoted on the grounds of protecting minorities that are not accepted or liked by the majority: from this perspective, the problem is the dislike of certain minority groups that leads to intolerance, the antidote to which is tolerance. As Galeotti states:

> So what differences between which groups constitute the circumstances in which toleration is called for? In general, toleration is needed when certain groups are 'different' in ways which are disliked by the majority in a society . . . the groups in question have to be genuinely dislike.[14]

The usage of toleration as a form of enlightened attitude towards groups now dominates the literature, to the extent that Williams can confidently assert: 'basically, toleration is a matter of the attitudes of any group to another'. In its colloquial usage it serves as an antonym to bigotry and prejudice regarding 'human relations and of the attitude of one way of life toward another'.[15] The advocacy organization Teaching Tolerance 'is dedicated to reducing prejudice, improving intergroup relations and supporting equitable school experiences'.[16] In this way tolerance is reinvented as an educational doctrine for conveying moral truths. The very act of associating tolerance with any cause or value communicates the warning that it is beyond debate, since only the intolerant would question it. Far from serving as a testing ground for the clarification of ideas, in its capacity as an educational doctrine tolerance is called upon to highlight views that are beyond discussion. As a study of the Swedish core school curriculum notes, tolerance is taught as a fundamental virtue, whose status is 'indisputable', 'non-negotiable' and not 'objects for compromise'.[17] In this way the rhetorical positioning of tolerance towards an object invites intolerance towards its critics.

In principle, it is entirely legitimate to revise, develop or elaborate a philosophical or political idea such as tolerance. However the adoption of a different or novel interpretation of a concept requires that it be explicitly justified. In particular it demands that the author of the new concept indicates the extent to which it is consistent or inconsistent with its previous usage. J. S. Mill, for example, took the idea of tolerance in a new direction and extended its meaning to encompass the idea of 'social tolerance'. Mill's *On Liberty* drew attention to what he characterized as the 'tyranny of public opinion', by which he meant non-legal forms of social disapproval, pressure and ostracism. Mill's concern with social intolerance was motivated by the fear that the mores and customs of majority opinion could acquire the capacity to impose a conformist cultural climate on individuals holding dissident or radical opinions. His focus on social intolerance was influenced by the recognition that minority opinion was necessary to question the unreflected certainties of mainstream society.

Some traditionalists and conservatives find it difficult to understand and accept Mill's concern about the potentially suffocating influence of received customs and opinion. Mill has been criticized for advocating tolerance for views and forms of behaviour that traditionalists find abhorrent, and it is argued that his openness to dissident view and behaviour represents an abdication of moral responsibility.[18] Yet Mill's concern with social intolerance was underwritten by his conviction that a community's unexamined truths needed to account for themselves to avoid turning into dogma. The influence exercised by such powerful opinion could lead to the suppression of unconventional views, thereby losing an important opportunity for clarifying ideas. But it was not only the demands of epistemological tolerance that motivated Mill to limit the power of majority opinion: it was also the realization that the influence of unquestioned, majority-sanctioned conventions could constrain individuals from exercising their autonomy. From this perspective the principal argument for the restraint of social intolerance is the necessity of protecting individual autonomy from its baleful influence.

Mill's concept of social intolerance represents a logical extension of the liberal conceptualization of the problem. From this perspective he outlines an open-minded orientation to pluralism and diversity of opinions. However, there is a fundamental difference between a commitment to the acceptance of

pluralism in relation to different ways of life and the current
usage of tolerance as an instrument for managing group relations. In Mill's case the objective was to create the condition
for people to choose for themselves beliefs and ways of life in
accordance with their experience and inclination. The current
commitment to the toleration of groups, by contrast, does not
involve any particular attachment either to the clarification
of opinion or to the exercise of individual autonomy. Indeed
the very pursuit of group toleration often communicates the
assumption that, rather than possessing the capacity for autonomy, individuals exist as the personification of group culture
and experience.

Wolff draws attention to the paradoxical tendency of
American pluralism to combine its calls for tolerance towards
different ethnic groups with illiberalism towards non-
conventional views and behaviour. The paradox is all the more
interesting in that it draws attention to a contradiction between
America as the land of individual opportunity and the tendency
to regard individuals as possessing the attitudes and attributes
of their cultural background. The assumption of pluralism,
argues Wolff, is that individuals belong to a group and will
'internalize the values' of their community. Consequently, the
tolerance accorded to people is in their capacity as members of
their group rather than in relation to their individual beliefs and
views. American culture is thus able to tolerate different religions, but not individuals who are not religious. Wolff claims
that the 'greatest tolerance' is for 'established groups' along
with 'an equally great intolerance for the deviant individual'.[19]
As a result in the 1940s, 1950s and 1960s the flourishing of
American pluralism could coexist with intolerance towards
atheists, beatniks, and communists, as well those who adopted
unconventional ways of living.

Since the 1960s the tendency to perceive people as possessing identities that are cultural rather than the outcome of individual accomplishment has gained significant momentum. From this perspective individuals are tolerated as members of a particular group rather than because of their individual beliefs or actions. Underpinned by the outlook of cultural pluralism, personal beliefs and opinions have become disassociated from individual reflection and conscience, and become expressions of pre-given cultural identities. As Brown observes, this 'formulation stands in significant contrast to the Lockean notion that beliefs are matters of personal revelation or deliberation in which our agentic individuality is the expression of our fundamental humanness'. She concludes that from this standpoint, 'subject formation expresses our humanness as a cultural, ethnic, or sexual being and not as a choosing or thinking – free individual'.[20] An implicit cultural determinism endows people with an identity that defines then who they are. That is why identity is frequently represented as a fact of life that one is born with, rather than a matter of choice. In its most extreme form identity becomes entirely naturalized – homosexuality, for example, is viewed not as a choice influenced by sexual desire but as the inexorable consequence of a so-called gay gene. The claim that it is a genetic disposition that accounts for one's sexuality represents a response to the attempt to stigmatize it as 'unnatural'. But in the very act of naturalizing identity the human capacity for autonomy and choice is diminished.

The recasting of tolerance into a narrative of group rights is part of a wider cultural tendency that holds culture, ethnicity or sexuality as the determinants of people's consciousness and identity. The fossilization of identity accomplished through ascribing individual consciousness to the working of culture offers an account of personhood that is bereft of human agency. The individual enters the stage as the personification of a cultural fact. In this role the individual is dispossessed of the capacity for self-reflection and self-determination. The toleration of such culturally enforced identities has little in common with the liberal meaning of the term. Tolerance is rendered banal, becoming an expression of an etiquette of polite society. If an inherited identity trumps individual choice, moral autonomy ceases to have meaning.

The concept of tolerance needs to be rescued from its current illiberal usage. It should therefore not be applied to encompass the management of inter-group relations. It is legitimate to use the concept of tolerance in relation to groups that are bound together by religion, opinion or ideology, but in that case tolerance refers to the beliefs and views held by members of that group. One can and should tolerate Judaism, the Islamic faith, and Queer politics – one cannot and should not 'tolerate' Jews, Muslims, or homosexuals on the basis of their group identity. Although communal, ethnic and religious conflicts represent a significant threat to humanity, the way to approach this problem is not through the application of tolerance to the management of group conflicts. Democratic theory upholds the right of self-determination and insists on the non-discriminatory application of civil rights. In addition to the protection of the civil liberties of different groups, a democratic society also attempts to create institutions where social harmony can be promoted. Jews, Muslims or homosexuals do not need toleration, they need their rights to be protected and upheld.

Every democratic society is confronted with the challenge of tackling the problem of social cohesion. However, it is wrong to imagine that an idea that was developed specifically to deal with conflicts expressed through religion and belief is also useful for resolving animosities and disputes that are national, racial and cultural. Tolerance is not an all-purpose antidote to every form of prejudice and conflict. One fundamental difference between responding to a conflict over ethnic affiliation as opposed to belief is the attitude to the other party. The tolerance of a particular religion or opinion does not mean their acceptance: it is precisely because of our disagreement or disapproval of a particular belief that we are called upon to tolerate. We don't tolerate our own opinions or those in agreement with ours.

Tolerance is based on the prior acts of reflection, judgement and discrimination. That is why opinions that we tolerate are also ones with which we disagree. The same standards of discrimination and judgement ought not be applied to cultural, ethnic or racial groups, because a liberal democratic ethos is inconsistent with the idea of discriminating between people on ethnic, racial or cultural grounds. So from a liberal or democratic perspective, people's right to equal treatment needs to be accepted, not tolerated.

Whether group rights are accepted, celebrated or rejected is in any case a practical question that depends on the nature of the relationship among them. In principle, from a democratic standpoint one can, in some circumstances, argue for the acceptance and protection of group rights while contesting them in different contexts. Although a mature democratic society will be sensitive and open-minded to requests for allowing groups certain cultural rights in some cases, it can legitimately reject such demands. Protecting and affirming cultural identities may well reinforce natural and social differences and conflict, and a government may legitimately adopt the view that in the interest of social integration it is preferable to adopt policies that diminish the significance of such identities.

The attempt to expand the concept of tolerance to the governing of group conflicts is unlikely to provide a successful resolution to the problem. Groups, be they cultural, ethnic or lifestyle groups, do not simply want to be tolerated, they want to be respected and treated as the moral equivalents of everyone else. It is precisely because tolerance evokes ideas to do with judgement and discrimination that minority groups regard it suspiciously as a gesture that is designed to appease them. Critics of the concept of tolerance often draw on this point and go on to draw the conclusion that 'mere' tolerance is not enough.

In a roundabout way the expansion of the meaning of toleration reduces it to a shallow gesture that can easily be dismissed as a form of cynical or tokenistic behaviour. This deprives the concept of any inherent virtue and makes it easily misinterpreted as an instrument of cultural domination towards those whom we deem our inferiors. Writing in this vein, Griffin writes that toleration involves judgement that begins with a 'sense of objection to something inferior'.[21] Brown echoes this sentiment, when she writes that the current discourse on tolerance involves 'the marking of subjects of tolerance as inferior, deviant, or marginal'.[22] Others argue that those who are tolerated are also not liked and made to feel unwelcome: Galeotti contends that toleration 'exhibits a particularly problematic aspect: if its precondition is the presence of conflicting social differences, this implies that the bearers of such differences do not welcome what they see as being incompatible with their views and forms of life'.[23]

If tolerance is perceived as a pragmatic instrument for conflict resolution, it is not surprising that advocates of identity and politics will tend to portray it as a cynical and opportunist tool for evading the problem. Arguing in this vein, Tariq

Ramadan insists that tolerance represents an act of evasion – a way of avoiding contact with those whom we find troubling. He writes that this approach leads to the elaboration of 'great and beautiful philosophies of tolerance and pluralism', which masquerade as 'a highly virtual petition of generosity' but in fact represent 'an extremely subtle way of avoiding the need to be open-minded'.[24] According to this interpretation, tolerance represents an act of hypocrisy and expresses the outlook of those who make a 'show of being anti-racist' while avoiding contact with blacks, Arabs and Asians.

If one accepts the conceptual shift of tolerance from individual belief to that of group rights, the kind of objections raised by Ramadan retain a measure of validity. But that is to misunderstand the concept of tolerance, perceiving it as an instrument for validating group identity. The attempt to reconstitute tolerance as an attitude that eschews judgement, however, turns a fine ideal linked to liberty and freedom into a therapeutic act of affirmation.

The transformation of an empirical fact into a moral virtue

The banalization of tolerance acquires its apotheosis with its linkage to diversity. In recent decades the word 'diversity' has mutated from an empirical fact into a moral ideal.[25] This word was once used to describe variations of life, and the *Oxford English Dictionary* still defines diversity as 'the condition or quality of being diverse, different, or varied'. It is a condition of unlikeness that points to a normal feature of both the biological and the social world. As such, the word 'diversity', like the words 'distinction', 'variety' or 'many', expresses a fact of life rather than a normative proposition about virtue.

Yet today, advocates of identity politics, mainstream parliamentary parties, educators, and a variety of moral entrepreneurs constantly demand that we value diversity and that children are taught the virtue of tolerating it. With the ascendancy of identity politics and multiculturalism, diversity and its companion term, difference, have acquired the status of indisputable moral virtues in themselves. This rhetorical leap from a description of life to an object of veneration resembles the fetishization of natural objects in ancient cultures and religions: people are not simply expected to live with the variations of human life but also to worship them.

As Brown writes, 'difference itself is what students learn they must tolerate'.[26] Children are taught to tolerate difference as something important for its own sake rather than to tolerate a particular view or a specific form of behaviour. Conversely, pupils are instructed that 'intolerance of differenceis at the roots of most violence.[27] From the perspective of this platitudinous formulation, differences in hair colour, variations in lifestyle, and deadly ethnic rivalry between people can be captured through the same concept. Books with titles like *Tolerance and Education*, *Learning to Live with Diversity and Difference*, *Diversity and Tolerance in Socio-Legal Contexts*, *Helping Students Learn the Value of Tolerance*, *Diversity and Inclusion* and *Debating Diversity: Analysing the Discourse of Tolerance* testify to the close connection and the symbiotic relationship between tolerance and diversity. The relationship between tolerance, diversity and difference has become so intimate that contemporary public rhetoric often uses the terms interchangeably. Use of the term diversity as a sacred moral principle is not confined to earnest apologists for political correctness: businesses and public sector organizations declare its virtues in their mission statements. When the World Bank organizes 'Diversity and Tolerance Workshops' it is evident that diversity has become truly sacralized.[28]

In current parlance, it often appears that tolerance draws its moral status from its capacity to uphold and celebrate diversity. Although the discourse surrounding tolerance, diversity and difference is incoherent and rarely accounts for itself in a morally literate language, it is evident that diversity is a first-order principle that demands attitudes and forms of behaviour associated with tolerance. The transformation of diversity from an empirically given fact to a moral value is rarely the subject of conscious reflection, yet it is far from evident why 'different' possesses inherent virtues that are lacking in the 'same'.

The sacralization of diversity is more an outcome of political pragmatism and calculation than of moral reflection. In recent decades, numerous Western societies have found it difficult to give meaning to national unity. In the absence of a working consensus about the meaning of a way of life, many societies have become far more conscious of the influences that divide them than those that unite them. In such circumstances politicians and cultural elites find it difficult to talk the language of national unity, can rarely find words that can inspire minorities to assimilate, and struggle to explain what it is that binds people together.

Instead of elaborating a public ethos that can guide and inspire a community, people are exhorted to celebrate diversity. In this form, as a politically constructed value, diversity is used to communicate the idea of accepting and respecting the different groups that inhabit society. Through the sacralization of diversity, society is spared the problem of having to deal with the difficult issues raised through confronting cultural and other divisions. A divided society is miraculously reborn as a diverse one, and tolerance is called upon to respect and celebrate it. When tolerance is used in this manner it loses its liberating potential for developing people through the exercise of their autonomy or helping to clarify the truth. It works as an instrument for helping to contain inter-group animosity and avoid drawing attention to the potentially corrosive effect of cultural disunity. As Brown observes, 'tolerance as a primary civic virtue and dominant political value entails a view of citizenship as passive and of social life as reduced to relatively isolated individuals or groups barely containing their aversion towards one another'.[29] One could add that once tolerance becomes implicated in the project of celebrating diversity, it becomes complicit in the fossilization of difference and identity.

The current multicultural discourse on tolerance actually distracts attention from the way that it can creatively interact with diversity. In his opening motto to *On Liberty*, Mill cites a passage from the German thinker Wilhelm von Humboldt's *Sphere and Duties of Government*:

> The grand, leading principle, towards which every argument unfolded in these pages directly converges, is the absolute and essential importance of human development in its richest diversity.

The significance that Mill attached to the development of the 'richest diversity' of human nature has little in common with its current usage. For Mill diversity signified variations in opinions and character, and the diversity of opinions served as a counterweight to the consolidation of received opinion and its transformation into a dogma. It should be stressed that when Mill used the term diversity it was in relation to individual difference rather than in the sense of cultural community-wide groups. Moreover, unlike the current sacralization of diversity,

Mill regarded variant views as not ends in themselves but as a means towards gaining greater clarity about the problems confronting humanity. In this respect, Mill was affirming a philosophical tradition that gained its first systematic expression with Socrates, who took people's opinions seriously because he believed that they contained potential truth waiting to unfold.

Because he held that humanity was not infallible, Mill believed that society required 'different opinions' and 'different experiments of living'.[30] He took the view that a diversity of human thought and conduct was necessary for the full development of the human potential. His was a point further developed by the political philosopher Hannah Arendt, who regarded the ability to understand other people's opinions through a dialogue as the principal task of public life. As one commentator observes, 'Arendt's persistent stress on human plurality and the sharing of diverse opinions' was for her the '*sine qua non* of any politics worthy of the name'.[31]

However, neither Arendt nor Mill upheld diversity as a value in its own right. Rather, they regarded diversity as means to attain a greater insight into the human condition. Mill believed that a 'gradual narrowing of the bounds of diversity of opinion' was an 'inevitable and indispensable' dimension of progress and intellectual development. Indeed, he went as far as to suggest that as 'mankind improves, the number of doctrines which are no longer disputed or doubted will be constantly on the increase: and the well-being of mankind may almost be measured by the number of and gravity of truths which have reached the point of being uncontested'.[32]

Today, Mill's view that the clash of diverse beliefs would eventually lead to a unanimity of views strikes one as symptomatic of the naive optimism of nineteenth-century progressives regarding the discovery of uncontested truths. However, regardless of our assessment of Mill's diagnosis of the future, his proposition about the creative potential for a diversity of views to take forward society's comprehension of the truth provides an important argument for tolerance. Mill's belief in the possibility that the contestation of conflicting views would eventually give way to consensus was in part influenced by an important tenet of progressive thought that took the view that, with the expansion of knowledge, uncertainty would give way to certainty.[33] The experience of history provides a more complicated picture. Debate and the clash of opinion do help to turn partial truths into more all-sided ones, but the very process of gaining greater certainty throws up new questions. Paradoxically, the more that we know, the more we are obliged to live with uncertainty. In a sense uncertainty is a constant feature of the human condition, requiring a positive attitude towards tolerating different beliefs and opinions.

Conclusion

While Mill regarded diversity as an instrument of intellectual and social experimentation necessary for tackling conformity, the current usage of this term is underwritten by a project that has the opposite objective. The exhortation to tolerate, or respect, diversity, demands not criticism or questioning but conformity. Since diversity is interpreted to mean respect for difference, anyone questioning this value courts the accusation of being disrespectful towards people of different cultures. Similarly if, as UNESCO argues, the definition of tolerance is 'harmony in difference', any doubts raised about the doctrine of valuing difference invite the charge of intolerance. The declaration of the United Nations on this point is categorical: its

1995 declaration on 'The Year of Tolerance' stated that tolerance was 'respect, acceptance and appreciation of the rich diversity of our world's cultures, our forms of expression and ways of being human'.[34]

Once diversity becomes a heavily loaded moral term it no longer has the capacity for encouraging a clash of conflicting opinions. Its function as received wisdom becomes not unlike the customs and values that served as the target of criticism of nineteenth-century liberals. Without judgement and discrimination, tolerance turns into an unquestioned form of culturally sanctioned behaviour. 'He who lets the world, or his portion of it, choose his plan for him, has no need of any other faculty than the ape-like one of imitation', observed Mill, accurately capturing the spirit that animates today's practitioners of formulaic tolerance.[35]

As noted in Chapter 4, the transformation of diversity into a moralized and absolute value logically leads to a fundamental revision of the idea of tolerance. Tolerance ceases to be an act of free will and serves as an instrument of moral conformity, taught in schools as an exercise of appropriate behaviour. Moral conformity and the fossilization of identity are the main cultural achievements of this type of toleration.

Our argument against the sacralization of diversity is inspired by a concern with which political culture has been impoverished by a rhetorical turn towards concepts that evade the process of public clarification of issues facing society. Our aim is not artificially to displace diversity with declarations of unity: the cultural divisions and clashes of lifestyles that influence the way we live cannot be overcome through well-meaning declarations of unity. From our standpoint it is not diversity as a fact of life that is the problem, but its exaltation as a moral virtue.

While governments use diversity as a value that spares them

the trouble of having to engage with problems thrown up by cultural disunity, advocates of identity politics regard diversity as a warrant for developing and affirming their lifestyles or ways of life. Ramadan believes that diversity undermines claims based on prevailing relations of power and represents a claim for equal respect. He writes that 'recognizing the diversity of paths and the equality of all human beings are the two preconditions for the respect that allows us to get beyond the power relationship characteristic of relations of tolerance'.[36] The transformation of toleration into an act of respect turns this concept into a therapeutic gesture – as one advocate notes, 'we view tolerance as a way of thinking and feeling'.[37] The psychological turn of the narrative of tolerance constitutes the subject matter of the next chapter.

Notes

1 Mill (2008), p. 26.
2 Edwards (1988), p. 90.
3 Edwards (1988), p. 107.
4 For a discussion of unknown unknowns, see Furedi (2007), chapter 3.
5 See Furedi (2004a), chapter 1.
6 See Jowit (2010).
7 See Furedi (2009), chapter 6 for a discussion of the current pedagogy of fatalism.
8 See Alleyne (2010).
9 See Thagard (2010).
10 Walzer (1997), p. 8.
11 Walzer (1997), p. 2.
12 Williams (1996), p. 19.
13 Wolff (1969), pp. 22–3.
14 Galeotti (2002), p. 88.
15 Williams (1996), p. 19.

16 See Teaching Tolerance: www.tolerance.org/about.
17 Orlenius (2008), p. 471.
18 See, for example, Stetson and Conti (2005), pp. 52 and 54.
19 Wolff (1969), p. 37.
20 Brown (2006), p. 43.
21 Griffin (2010), p. 27.
22 Brown (2006), p. 13.
23 Galeotti (2002), p. 20.
24 Ramadan (2010), pp. 40 and 41.
25 Some describe the celebration of diversity as an ideology. See Wood (2010).
26 Brown (2006), p. 16.
27 Brown (2006), p. 104.
28 See World Bank (2003).
29 Brown (2008), p. 88.
30 Mill (2008), p. 63.
31 Villa (2002), p. 15.
32 Mill cited in Canovan (1988), p. 178.
33 Nevertheless, as Urbinati (2002: 169) noted, Mill was aware that the lack of scientific certainty was 'inherent in the structure of human knowledge'.
34 Cited in Stetson and Conti (2005), p. 141.
35 Mill (2008), p. 65.
36 Ramadan (2010), p. 42.
37 See Teaching Tolerance: www.tolerance.org/about.

4

Tolerance Confused with Recognition

In its current usage, tolerance is often emptied of its association with freedom. Indeed it is frequently used in ways that contradict its capacity to reconcile critical judgement with the protection of dissident, even offensive, views. Yet without judgement tolerance turns into a formulaic response whose main merit is that it unquestioningly offers respect-on-demand to different groups and standpoints. It is necessary to question this confusion of tolerance with the disposition towards non-judgementalism. An act of tolerance does not signify respect to a culture, group or a single individual. Moreover, in some circumstances, such an act need not be inconsistent with sentiments such as disrespect, contempt and animosity towards a particular belief or opinion.

The call to 'respecting other people's opinions' outwardly appears as a sensible and courteous way of responding to differences. But granting respect to others' beliefs can have the effect of treating scientific knowledge and prejudice as equivalent. One of the ways that knowledge develops, and insights into truths are gained, is through rejecting and marginalizing views and sentiments founded on superstition and prejudice. In contemporary times the adoption of respect as a right has

78

the effect of restricting the open and uninhibited exchange of views in public life.

There is one important sense in which tolerance is closely connected to respect. Tolerance as moral virtue is intimately linked to the Kantian principle of respecting the human in virtue of being human. For Immanuel Kant (1724–1804) respect was oriented to people in their capacity as moral agents possessing the potential to live their lives in accordance with reasons and motives that were genuinely their own. In this sense that respect accorded to people in their capacity as autonomous individuals informs and motivates the liberal idea of tolerance. Both Kant's moral philosophy and Mill's principle of liberty are grounded in a shared respect for moral autonomy: a respect that is granted unconditionally. Tolerance demands that we curb our inclination to restrain the self-directed moral reasoning of others. However, there is no moral obligation to extend the respect accorded to the exercise of individual autonomy to the ensuing conclusion or belief.

The exercise of moral reasoning and choice-making involves acts of judgement. Moral concern with autonomy presupposes that the bearer of tolerance possesses distinct views and beliefs. In contrast to this classical liberal interpretation, the current dominant version of tolerance seeks to divest it from the act of judgement. In line with contemporary cultural norms tolerance is upheld as a morally neutral act of non-judgementalism.

Often tolerance is *mistakenly* used to imply a relaxed indifference to other people and their views. In its everyday usage tolerance is frequently represented as a marker of an open-minded attitude. In its idealized form this attitude is not only free from prejudice and bigotry but also from the inclination to judge. The implication of this sentiment is that anyone who bears a dislike of someone's values and beliefs but nevertheless defends their right to express such despised sentiments cannot be characterized as tolerant: Horton insists that 'the tolerant person is not a narrow-minded bigot who shows restraint'. Since the very idea of restraining one's negative evaluation implies a prior act of judgement, it ceases to have the positive qualities that classical liberalism has attached to it. In this instance, judgement itself is deemed inappropriate.

Horton claims the reluctance to judge represents the hallmark of tolerance. 'The tolerant person is not too judgemental toward others', he writes, adding that 'in becoming less judgemental a person becomes more tolerant'.[1] The claim that tolerance is expressed through the attitude of non-judgementalism has acquired the status of a conventional wisdom in the educational institutions of the Anglo-American world and the European Union (EU). This consensus is summed up by the Horten-like formula that a 'tolerant person is less judgemental towards others' and that 'in becoming less judgemental, a person becomes more tolerant'.[2]

Although non-judgementalism is represented as an enlightened and liberal attitude towards the world, it is nothing of the sort. Obviously, the unreflected judgements arrived at through stereotyping are merely manifestations of conformism and prejudice. But the valuation of non-judgementalism possesses no inherent positive ethical qualities. The reluctance to judge may be a symptom of disinterest or even moral cowardice. In current times it is often brought about by a reluctance to confront difficult and embarrassing questions. Not questioning others' beliefs and opinions closes the door to the elaboration of a mutually agreed public consensus.

Twenty-first-century Western society is so uncomfortable with making value judgements that it has developed an entire vocabulary of euphemisms to avoid being unambiguous, clear and blunt in its statements.[3] This trend is particularly visible in schooling and education, where a veritable Orwellian vocabulary has emerged to provide teachers and others with words that avoid judgement. In schools children are described as having 'special needs', or 'hard to reach', or 'gifted and talented'. Arendt characterizes the reluctance to judge as an expression of a disinclination towards public association and writes of the 'blind obstinacy that becomes manifest in the lack of imagination and failure to judge'.[4]

Non-judgementalism is often a masquerade for sneaking value judgements in through the back door. This is what Horton does when he describes a tolerant person as one who is not 'excessively judgmental, not too narrow-minded, not inappropriately moralistic'. His is clearly a statement of judgement about the characteristics of a tolerant person and, by implication, an intolerant one. Terms like 'narrow-minded' and 'inappropriate' are not ones of neutral description. This tendency to judge by inference is even clearer when Horton states that 'eliminating misplaced objections might also be seen as part of the value of tolerance'.[5] Here the verdict of 'objections' as 'misplaced' indicates that Horton has no problems about judging and morally indicting those who have the affront to judge.

From a liberal humanist perspective, judgement is not simply an acceptable response to other people's beliefs and behaviour: it is a public duty. It is through the act of judgement that a dialogue is established between an individual and others. Drawing on Kant's *Critique of Judgement*, Hannah Arendt writes of an 'enlarged way of thinking, which as judgement knows how to transcend its own individual limitations'. According to current conventional prejudice, the act of judging confines the imagination and encourages narrow-mindedness. In fact, as Arendt contends, judging plays a central role in disclosing to individuals the nature of their public world: 'judging is one, if not the most, important activity in which this sharing-the-world-with-others comes to pass'.[6] Judgement does not simply mean the dismissal of another person's belief: 'the power of judgement rests on a potential agreement with others'.[7] This is one compelling reason why true tolerance depends on judgement.

The positive potential of an act of judgement depends on the degree to which it is based on experience, reflection and impartiality. Not all judgements are of equal worth and, as Arendt remarks, the quality of a judgement 'depends upon the degree of its impartiality'.[8] But partial and hasty evaluations are not an argument against judging; only for adopting a more responsible attitude towards it.

Why has the creative public act of judgement become culturally devalued? To some extent the devaluation of the act of judgement is influenced by intellectual currents that are both sceptical of knowledge claims and argue that everyone's views ought to be respected. Such relativist currents often denounce people with strong views as 'essentialists' and 'fundamentalists'. A more important source for the devaluation of judgement is the ascendancy of what I have characterized as therapy culture.[9] From the standpoint of this cultural imagination, people are often perceived as lacking the capacity to engage with disappointment and criticism. In the US, the sentiment that 'criticism is violence' has gained significant influence over this nation's cultural elites.[10] Judgement is often portrayed as a form of psychic violence, especially if applied to children: the sociologist Richard Sennett writes of the 'devastating implications of rendering judgement on someone's future'.[11] However, in a complex society, it is impossible not to judge and compare. The institutionalization of diversity through pursuing policies that avoid judgement is partly an attempt to respond to this dilemma. But in the end, the gesture of not judging merely reinforces people's anxieties towards being judged.

The identification of tolerance with non-judgementalism is often expressed through treating both as an attitude or psychological disposition. In education and public affairs tolerance is often assumed to be an attitude that is more or less interchangeable with open-mindedness. In its form as an attitude, tolerance is turned into a personality trait that connotes a disposition towards acceptance of other people's culture, beliefs and behaviour. American social scientists have been in the forefront of transforming tolerance into a measurable, definable personality trait; as a psychological disposition tolerance 'became an inner-state that could be measured, cultivated and educated'.[12]

As an emotional attitude, tolerance speaks to the therapeutic turn of Western culture. It conveys not only the emotional disposition towards not judging and accepting, but also the therapeutic values associated with respecting and affirming. Often the criticism of 'mere tolerance' contains an implicit demand for respect, and there are powerful cultural forces that legitimize the usage of tolerance as an instrument for affirming, even celebrating, cultures and lifestyles. Increasingly, the ideal of tolerance has become confused with the therapeutic demand for recognition. The illiberal and potentially authoritarian consequences of this shift will be one of the main themes explored in this chapter.

The therapeutic turn

The historical re-routing of tolerance from the management of beliefs to the management of group relations has coincided with a growing tendency to represent identity as a cultural statement about the inner life of the self. As I argue elsewhere, identity in both its individual and group form is increasingly associated with the mental state of the self.[13] Through the emotionalization of identity, the relationship of the self with wider external points of reference has dramatically altered. External constraints over the conduct of the self in everyday life, be they in the form of communal expectations, moral codes and taboos, or social values, have diminished in significance. Therapy culture demands that individual self-esteem must be protected from negative influences such as criticism and judgement.

The transformation of validation into an obligation dictated by cultural norms has as its premise a radically novel interpretation of the meaning of personhood. The liberal ideal of moral autonomy has been displaced by the belief that people lack agency and the resilience to deal with disappointment and negative judgement. Current etiquette presumes that the identity of the self will be validated, not judged. That is one important reason why the act of judgement has given way to the therapeutic value of affirmation. It is also why tolerance is either redefined as a warrant for respect or deemed to be unfit for the current therapeutic age. Ramadan, for one, is prepared to renounce tolerance on this ground and replace it with respect. He believes that tolerance fails to recognize its recipients and does not nourish their identity, thus 'tolerance can reduce the other to a mere presence; respect opens up to us the complexity of his being'.[14]

Ramadan has the merit of being consistent in his approach to the idea of tolerance. Having recognized that tolerance treats its object as just that – its object – he opts for abandoning this ideal and embracing respect. Mendus also understands that the liberal idea of toleration is inconsistent with the therapeutic imperative of making people good about themselves.

Consequently, she counsels the adoption of a more inclusive model of tolerance, concluding:

> Yet the real damage done by both toleration and by intolerance is precisely the same. When people are the recipients of state toleration, they may feel as alienated from the wider society as they do when they are persecuted. The need which is felt by persecuted minorities is not a need which can be satisfied by liberal toleration – however extensive it may be. Such people demand respect, and esteem. They want to be welcomed and wanted. They want to feel that they belong.[15]

According to Mendus, both tolerance and intolerance have a similar psychological impact on people. This interpretation is based on widely accepted therapeutic cultural norms that presume that, unless people are respected and esteemed, they will be emotionally distressed, even damaged. If that is so, then the extension of respect becomes mandatory. The very reluctance to show respect is often characterized as a variant of unacceptable behaviour likely to inflict emotional damage on the non-respected.

In the course of promoting the project of cultural and identity formation, some of its advocates have opted to revise the concept of tolerance so that it works as the therapeutic affirmation of its recipient. This is the rhetorical strategy adopted by Galeotti, who wants tolerance to possess an 'encompassing conception of inclusion, one which takes into account and emphasizes the aspects of dignity, respect, and worth'.[16] This prescription is consistent with current norms that regard people's emotional state as peculiarly problematic and in need of respect, at the same time as it is constitutive of their identity. Unstable identities create both a craving and a demand for respect.

From this standpoint, the liberal attitude of tolerance and its project of liberty is far less relevant than the therapeutic act of group identity affirmation. 'If what is really at stake in contemporary issues of toleration is equal respect and social standing for minority groups rather than equal liberties for individuals', writes Galeotti, 'then the issue of public toleration must be addressed not simply in terms of the compatibility between liberal institutions and various culture or practices, but in terms of contests over the inclusion of distinct identities and their bearers in the polity via the public recognition of the differences'.[17] The notion of equality of respect turns recognition into a rhetorical gesture. When everybody and every belief are equally respected, no one is genuinely affirmed. As a standardized response, it echoes the cheerful 'have a nice day' rhetoric of fast food chains. Real respect is a far more complicated process, involving reflection on the behaviour and actions of its recipients, and it is as much earned as it is endowed.

The demand for recognition

The growing preoccupation with the politics of identity reflects a growing trend to perceive differences in cultural terms. This is what drives the demand for tolerance to assume the form of cultural affirmation and recognition. This redirection of tolerance towards cultural identity has an important influence on public life. As the American social commentator Jedediah Purdy remarks, 'identity politics, based on sex, sexuality, and, mostly, race and ethnicity, suggests that politics should work not so much to give people *things* such as education and jobs as to give them *recognition*.[18] The growth of identity politics and the claim for recognition has had a significant influence on

contemporary political discourse and policymaking. This preoccupation with identity has created a demand for recognition,
which in turn has contributed to the redefinition of tolerance
as a regime of affirmation for people's feelings.

Since the end of the Cold War, the politics of recognition has
been widely promoted as an enlightened alternative to previous
norms of justice claims. One of the advantages claimed on its
behalf is that it gives due recognition to the individual, since it
is directed 'at the particular qualities that characterize people
in their personal difference'.[19] Contemporary proponents of
the politics of recognition assume that it is that driven by a
deep psychological need: the self becomes actualized through
cultural identity. One of the most powerful advocates of this
thesis, the German philosopher Alex Honneth, adopts Donald
Winnicott's object-relations theory to promote a model where
psychological damage inflicted on the individual is represented
as the central problem of injustice and inequality.[20] The focus
of Honneth's concern is the psychological damage inflicted on
people by a society that fails to encourage the development of
their self-confidence, self-respect and self-esteem. 'The experience of being socially denigrated or humiliated endangers the
identity of human beings, just as infection with disease endangers their physical life', writes Honneth.[21]

From this therapeutic perspective, even indifference is interpreted as a form of non-recognition, which is why the liberal
idea of tolerance is rejected by proponents of the politics of
recognition. This demand for recognition is justified on the
ground that minorities and cultural groups whose collective
identity was disparaged in the past lack the confidence and
emotional resources to assume the role of active citizens. Such
people need to feel that they are valued and respected if they are
to overcome their emotional deficit. At this point the hypocrisy

of non-judgementalism becomes unstuck: for what is really required is a positive verdict.

For Galeotti, positive affirmation is obligatory because 'the feeling of shame, humiliation, and self-hatred experienced in connection with their differences, reinforced by the required public invisibility of their identity, prevents people from developing an adequate level of self-respect and self-esteem, both of which are necessary for developing a voice and for making it heard, as well as for enjoying rights and for participating fully in the polity'.[22] In accordance with the duty to affirm, Galeotti calls for a 'general revision of the concept of toleration', which is 'tolerance as recognition'. This involves a 'semantic extension from the negative meaning of non-interference to the positive sense of acceptance and recognition'.[23]

The demand for the right to be esteemed has troubled some of the theorists of recognition. Francis Fukuyama is concerned that the automatic granting of esteem avoids the making of moral choices about what deserves to be esteemed. He notes that the 'problem with the present-day self-esteem movement is that its members . . . are seldom willing to make choices concerning what should be esteemed'.[24] Nancy Fraser argues that the view 'that everyone has an equal right to social esteem' renders 'meaningless the notion of esteem'.[25] However, once the right to recognition is accepted as a defining feature of a just society, it becomes difficult to place conditions on the automatic granting of esteem to every person regardless of their specific traits, accomplishments or contributions.

Ironically, the institutionalization of the right to recognition necessarily leads to emptying it of any moral content. Human struggles for recognition are mediated through specific historical and cultural forms. Such struggles often contain a creative dynamic of making history, enhancing self-consciousness, making moral choices, entering into dialogues, and accomplishing the construction of identities organic to one's circumstances. Struggling for recognition involves a different process to gaining recognition on demand. The former involves an active engagement of construction; the latter implies being acted upon by those conferring recognition. Such a right can never satisfy the craving to be recognized – it merely incites the individual to demand more assurances of respect. However, the very act of offering respect to those who crave it may make matters more complicated. The sociologist Richard Sennett suggests that the weak may quite rightly experience the extension of such respect as an empty gesture or, worse still, as ritual confirming their position of inferiority.[26] Instead of providing a solution, the institutionalization of recognition inadvertently encourages individuals and groups to develop an addiction for respect that can never be satisfied.

The legitimation of intolerance

Contemporary culture's commitment to recognizing and esteeming the individual contains a profoundly anti-individualistic dynamic. Recognition, as cultural-political norm and a state-sanctioned right, is consistent with the bureaucratic imperative of treating the individual according to an impersonal general formula. Despite its individualistic orientation, therapeutic intervention such as counselling often leads to the pursuit of the standardization of people rather than encourage a self-determined individuality. Recognition on demand overlooks individual differences and needs, and fails to distinguish between achievement and failure, wisdom and ignorance. A real recognition of the individual requires that choices are made between knowledge and opinion, and between contributions that are worth esteeming and those that are not. The demand and the granting of universal esteem cannot meet the existential quest for recognition. It can merely divert energy from constructive social engagement towards the quest for more institutional guarantees.

The very demand for the right to be esteemed posits a uniquely feeble version of the self. In effect it represents the negation of the idea of moral autonomy, placing the individual in a permanent position of supplicant, whose identity relies on rituals of bureaucratic affirmation. The self is not so much affirmed or realized but institutionally processed and given the bureaucratic equivalent of a smiley face. Wendy Brown describes the 'language of recognition' as the language of 'unfreedom', because of 'its impulse to inscribe in the law and in other political registers its historical and present pain rather than conjure an imagined future of power to make itself'.[27] Here autonomy, an essential component of human dignity, is exchanged for the quick fix of an institutionally affirmed identity.

The demand for recognition is not simply a request for sensitive and polite behaviour. It is integral to an etiquette of conformism that does not baulk at adopting illiberal political and institutional practices to realize its objectives. Increasingly, the provision of recognition is represented as not just an ethical but a legal obligation. Both public and private institutions have adopted formal and informal codes and practices that have as their objective the granting of automatic affirmation. The sentiment of prejudice, dislike and hate has become criminalized and a new genre of hate crimes that punish people for their beliefs has become institutionalized in numerous Western societies.

The invention of these new crimes is premised on the assumption that what people believe, what they communicate, and how they behave towards others, is likely to cause intense psychological damage. Mari Matsuda, a proponent of so-called critical race theory, argues for the criminalizing of racist speech on the grounds of its psychological impact on people: she describes such speech as 'assaultive speech' whose impact on 'one's self-esteem and sense of personal security is devastating'.[28]

The dramatization of the harms caused by criticism has encouraged the fantasy of imagining offensive language to be the equivalent of physical violence. Speech not only 'assaults' – in some cases, as with a racist slur, words become 'bullets'. As Rauch warns, the criminalization of offensive speech leads 'to the erasure of the distinction, in principle and ultimately also in practice, between discussion and bloodshed'.[29]

According to the inventors of the idea of assaultive speech, people who have fragile identities need to be protected from exposure to words and attitudes that will hurt them. Protecting people from such pain requires censorship and the micro-policing of intra-group attitudes and relations. When these censorious attitudes are fused with the imperative of recognition and validation, they invariably lead to the demand for intolerance of inappropriate sentiments. In many cases the demand for 'zero tolerance' for particular words or attitudes are justified on the ground that people's identity needs to be recognized and protected. Censorship is frequently legitimized on the grounds that it is indispensable for affirming and recognizing minorities. Numerous advocates argue that censorship communicates a symbolic message and offers a gesture of validation for people with weak identities. Invariably this argument colludes with a self-conscious attempt to argue for a targeted form of intolerance.

Proponents of recognition politics even go so far as to make a distinction between legitimate and illegitimate types of intolerance. One illustration of this adoption of a double standard towards tolerance is the distinction that Canadian political scientist Allison Harell draws between what she calls 'inclusionary intolerance' and 'exclusionary intolerance'. By exclusionary intolerance she refers to forms of disparaging conduct and words that destabilize people's identity, preventing them from feeling able to express themselves. In contrast, 'inclusionary intolerance arises in circumstances where minority groups are trying to fully participate in society by restricting the expression of prejudice directed at them'. In such instance 'inclusionary intolerance involves restricting the rights of the intolerant'.[30] She claims that intolerance directed towards the intolerant is 'democratically defensible' to secure the full participation of people who would otherwise feel excluded.

The application of a double standard towards intolerance is paralleled by the debasement of tolerance as a moral value. Those who regard the selective application of intolerance as a legitimate method for dealing with hateful ideas also tend to adopt an instrumental interpretation of tolerance. Harell argues that 'political tolerance should not be conceptualized as a binary concept where one is either intolerant or tolerant'.[31] The purpose of extinguishing a clear-cut distinction between tolerance and intolerance is to diminish the moral status of the former. Accordingly, the application of tolerance becomes contingent on the degree to which views and beliefs are regarded as objectionable. Tolerance turns into a moral good that is rationed according to circumstances. This selective and instrumental attitude towards tolerance is enthusiastically adopted by those claiming recognition rights.

Galeotti, like Harell, believes in the cause of fighting different forms of intolerance: for example, fighting racism with intolerance. They both adopt the tactic of regarding tolerance as a good that ought to be rationed out to signal approval or disapproval of people's behaviour. The rationing of tolerance is justified on the ground that, since the intolerant do not endorse the values of a tolerant society, they ought not enjoy its benefit. A more illiberal version of this argument states that since a tolerant society is at risk from the forces of intolerance, it is obliged to defend itself by whatever means necessary. Galeotti adopts such an argument for withholding toleration from those practising racist speech:

> The more tolerant a society, the more liberal it is, but also the more exposed to the risk of being overtaken by intolerant forces. If liberalism is to be preserved, toleration must be restricted: and the stricter its limits of toleration, the safer liberalism, but the less liberal the society.[32]

The claim that the preservation of liberalism depends on the careful rationing of toleration is frequently supported by campaigns for recognition.

Arguments that promote recognition through promoting intolerance towards the intolerant views of their opponents invariably justify their claim on the grounds of a trade-off between respect and freedom of speech. The legal scholar Owen Fiss contends that the policing of hate speech 'forces the legal system to choose between transcendent commitments – liberty and equality'. The belief that equality requires a trade-off against freedom is echoed by a leading advocate of censorship, the feminist writer Catharine MacKinnon, who states that when 'equality is mandated, racial and sexual epithets, vilification and abuse should also be prohibited'.[33] From this perspective, censoring the views and speech of those who inflict psychological pain on their target audience is a small price to pay for upholding the status of equality of respect.

The rationing of tolerance is founded on the assumption that a consistent and unwavering commitment to tolerance and free speech clashes with, and undermines, human dignity. This is the argument adopted by the political theorist Bhiku Parekh to justify the banning of 'hate speech'. Parekh accepts that 'free speech is an important value', but states that 'it is not the only one'. He counterposes the value of free speech to that of human dignity and insists that 'since these values conflict, either inherently or in particular contexts, they need to be balanced'. For Parekh, tolerance and freedom of speech ought not to be perceived as stand-alone principles which are inherently valuable. Their moral worth is relative, which is why 'free speech needs to be balanced against other great political values'.[34]

Since modern times began, assertions about the necessity of trading off freedoms for an alleged benefit have been used by critics of liberty, and these benefits have turned out to be illusory. However, the belief that human dignity and the sense of self-worth requires protection from the pain inflicted by hurtful speech is possibly the most counterproductive example of the trade-off argument. People acquire dignity and esteem through dealing with the problems that confront them, rather than through relying on the good will of the censor or the police.

Trading off freedom for some alleged psychic benefit is not unlike the argument that authoritarian-minded politicians frequently employ for justifying policies that curb people's rights in order to 'preserve their freedom'. Time and again intolerance appears as a weapon of choice by those who claim to defend the values of a tolerant society. As one commentator in the *Wall Street Journal* states:

The true complexity arises when we must defend these values in a world that does not universally embrace them – when we reach the place where we must be intolerant in order to defend tolerance, or unkind in order to defend kindness, or hateful in order to defend what we love.[35]

Attempting to defend tolerance by restricting it when confronted by those who are intolerant conveys the impression that tolerance is best protected by adopting the moral standards of its enemies. Not only is this posture illogical, it deprives tolerance of any principled moral content. As Dworkin argues, 'in a culture of liberty' the public 'shares a sense, almost as a matter of secular religion, that certain freedoms are in principle exempt' from the 'ordinary process of balancing and regulation'. He fears that 'liberty is already lost' as 'soon as old freedoms are put at risk in cost-benefit politics'.[36]

Many intelligent observers have raised concerns about the ease with which political leaders have been able to win the public's acquiescence to their demand that security be traded for freedom, through policies designed to curb the speech and activities of those deemed the enemy. However, when a similar trade-off is proposed in relation to limiting tolerance towards offensive speech in order to validate or celebrate a particular lifestyle, such criticism is conspicuous by its absence.

Western culture's willingness to accept the rationing of tolerance in order to protect people and groups from offence represents a significant threat to the freedom of thought. The Rushdie affair, which erupted in February 1989, demonstrated the disquieting consequences of the loss of cultural support for liberal tolerance. When the Ayatollah Ruhollah Khomeini issued a fatwa against the novelist Salman Rushdie, far too many public figures wavered and refused to be counted.

Numerous members of the cultural elites decried the threat while also arguing that Rushdie should not have written a novel that insulted Islam, and Rushdie was accused of 'abusing' free speech. As one liberal critic of this display of moral cowardice writes:

> The Rushdie affair was a defining moment. It showed how readily Westerners could be backed away from a fundamental principle of intellectual liberalism, namely that there is nothing wrong with offending – hurting people's feelings – in pursuit of the truth.[37]

Once the recognition of difference trumps the right to judge and criticize, it is only a matter of time before the appearance of the censor.

The situation since the Rushdie affair has gone from bad to worse. The ascendancy and institutionalization of the politics of recognition has led to a proliferation of formal and informal codes that aim to outlaw offending people's feelings. In all but name, the cultural premise of the fatwa against Rushdie – if not the actual death sentence – has become accepted as a guide to life. The sociologist Tariq Madood states that 'if people are to occupy the same political space without conflict, they mutually have to limit the extent to which they subject each others' fundamental beliefs to criticism'.[38] The widespread acquiescence to the idea that in a pluralistic democracy the tolerance of conflicting views and opinions needs to be curbed and policed highlights the precarious status of freedom.

In the twenty-first century it is no longer necessary for a Middle Eastern theocrat to issue a fatwa for a book to be banned. The fate of the novel *The Jewel of Medina* provides a cautionary tale of craven self-censorship. The novel, originally bought by the publisher Random House, was sent to Denise Spellberg, an associate professor of Islamic history at the University of Texas, for comment and endorsement. When Spellberg denounced the book as 'offensive', Random House dropped the title from its list.[39] If one offended university teacher can prevent the publication of a novel, it is not surprising that policing offensive behaviour has become a growth industry. The illiberal laws passed against incitement of religious hatred in the post-9/11 era is testimony to a growing momentum behind the rationing of tolerance.

The confusion of tolerance with recognition transforms an idea associated with the pursuit of freedom to one that actively discourages open discussion and criticism. Recognition depends on the unquestioned validation of the recipients of respect. Numerous institutions, businesses and public sector bodies insist that their members or employees sign up to the ethos of recognition. For example AT&T Broadband in the US demands that its new employees sign a 'Certificate of Understanding' to affirm that they agree with the policies and rules of the company. One such policy states that 'each person at AT&T Broadband is charged with the responsibility to fully recognize, respect and value the differences among all of us'.[40] Employees are not simply asked to tolerate, but told to respect and value, lifestyles that may well be antithetical to their own.

The institutionalization of recognition has profoundly disturbing implications for liberalism. It represents a regime that informs people what to believe and how to think, and also how to feel towards other people and groups. This process is a series of steps that begins with not judging, moves into respecting, and eventually leads to validating and celebrating the subjects of recognition. In this scenario there is little scope for the exercise of autonomy and acting in accordance with one's conscience. The feeble cultural support for autonomy leads to the undermining of the authority of freedom of speech and belief.

Notes

1 Horton (1996), p. 38.
2 Burwood and Wyeth (1998), p. 468.
3 This point will de developed in our discussion on speech codes and the policing of words.
4 Hannah Arendt 'Truth and politics', in Arendt (2006), p. 237.
5 Horton (1996), p. 41.
6 Hannah Arendt 'The crisis in culture', in Arendt (2006), pp. 217–18.
7 Arendt (2006), p. 217.
8 Arendt (2006), p. 237.
9 Furedi (2004b), chapter 1.
10 Rauch (1993), p. 6.
11 Sennett (2003), p. 98.
12 See Weissberg (1998), p. 10.
13 Furedi (2004b), chapter 7.
14 Ramadan (2010), p. 48.
15 Mendus (1989), p. 159.
16 Galeotti (2002), p. 97.
17 Galeotti (2002), p. 6.
18 Purdy (1999), p. 64.
19 See Honneth (1995), p. 122.
20 See Honneth (1995), p. 167.
21 Honneth (1995), p. 135.
22 Galeotti (2002), p. 9.
23 Galeotti (2002), p. 10.
24 Fukuyama (1992), p. 303.
25 Fraser (1998), p. 24.
26 Sennett (2003).
27 Brown (1995), p. 66.
28 Matsuda et al. (1993), p. 25.

29 Rauch (1993), p. 131.
30 Harell (2010), pp. 410–11.
31 Harell (2010), p. 412.
32 Galeotti (2002), p. 143.
33 See Fiss (1998), p. 13; and MacKinnon (1993), p. 71.
34 Parekh (2006), pp. 216 and 220.
35 Klavan (2008).
36 Dworkin (1996), p. 354.
37 Rauch (1993), p. 22.
38 Cited in Malik (2008).
39 For a discussion of this controversy, see Crawley (2008).
40 Von Bergen and Bandow (2010), p. 3.

5

The Expansion of the Meaning of Harm

Those who claim that recognition is a right also take the view that no tolerance should be shown towards those whose words and behaviour threaten to destabilize people's identity. This claim for rationing tolerance is warranted on the premise that it is essential to protect people from suffering psychic injury. Advocates insist that those whose speech and behaviour inflict harm should face legal sanctions. Moreover, the claim for recognition also maintains that restraining certain types of speech is vital for protecting vulnerable identities and affirming individuals and groups. While the restriction of tolerance due of its putative therapeutic benefits manifestly represents an illegitimate restraint on people's freedom, it is worth posing the question of what are the grounds, if any, for curbing people's freedom?

Mill attempted to provide an answer through his formulation of the well-known 'harm principle'. Mill argued that individual adults should be free to act in accordance with their inclinations so long as they did not harm another person, and that the protection of the individual from the harm caused by others is the sole justification for using coercion to restrain a person's liberty. Mill was categorical that the only valid argument for 'interfering with the liberty of action' of people is 'self-protection', and wrote that 'the only purpose for which power can be rightfully exercised over any member of a civilized community, against his will, is to prevent harm to others'.[1] The motive behind the elaboration of the harm principle was not to draw a boundary around the exercise of freedom so much as to offer a philosophical case for its safeguard. Compared to previous views on tolerance, the harm principle actually widens people's right to live their lives as they choose.

Until Mill's contribution to the debate, tolerance tended to be associated with the Lockean formulation, with its focus on the protection of religious belief. Mill took tolerance beyond this, and *On Liberty* unequivocally came out against any restriction on the communication and discussion of any doctrine and opinion 'however immoral it may be considered'. The content of speech, as such, could never provide a warrant for its suppression. The only restriction on speech that Mill was prepared to entertain was when it turned into a direct incitement to harm another person physically. His unqualified support for free speech was motivated by the significance he attached to the capacity of the exercise of individual autonomy to contribute to human flourishing. At the same time, Mill believed that if government had the power to curb people's belief and speech, people's autonomy would significantly diminish.

Mill went beyond Locke in calling not just for the toleration of beliefs but also for practices associated with them, taking the view that only practices that harm others should be the subject of government regulation. Beattie explains:

It is the move to the harm principle – extending our notion of tolerance to include the right of individuals to act out, and on, their interests and excluding the moral distress of citizens as grounds for political regulation – that will best achieve the conditions necessary for individual autonomy to flourish.[2]

Mill's extension of the idea of tolerance is animated by the belief that putting up with insults, lies, and dangerous and immoral opinions, is a small price to pay for the flourishing of autonomy and the intellectual and social benefits of open debate.

Mill's harm principle is antithetical to the present-day demands to curb speech on grounds of protecting people from offence or psychic distress. Mill does not deny that words can hurt: as Edwards comments, he in 'no way palliates' his argument 'by recourse to any feeble plea that opinions cannot be harmful'.[3] However, Mill took the view that the open exchange of opinion is necessary to create the conditions for the flourishing of moral independence. From his standpoint, moral distress does not constitute a 'harm warranting government intervention or regulation'.[4] It was his consistent commitment to the moral value of individual autonomy that lay behind Mill's insistence that, except to prevent imminent harm, government should refrain from regulating people's lives.

The inflation of harm

Since Mill developed his arguments *On Liberty*, the harm principle has been a constant subject of debate. His critics often claim that Mill's concept of harm is confusing: 'Unless we know what Mill means by "harm", we cannot usefully apply his principle', writes John Gray.[5] In contrast to Mill, who attempted to restrict the meaning of the harms that government could restrict, his critics tend to be more interested in expanding the definition of harm. Mill is very rarely criticized for not taking his idea of tolerance further: his detractors invariably query his unambiguous attachment to freedom.

One strategy adopted to discredit *On Liberty* is to argue that, whatever merits this essay may have possessed in the past, we live in a far more complicated world where free debate does not automatically lead to the discovery of the truth. The contention that the world has fundamentally changed relieves the critic of the responsibility to provide a frontal challenge to Mill's principle of liberty. An example of this approach is offered by the academic philosopher Nigel Warburton, who reminds his readers that 'Mill's model of the arena in which discussion takes place' is 'something like an idealized seminar with opinions calmly delivered on each side and truth emerging victorious and invigorated from its collision with error'.[6] The purpose of this caricature is to suggest that in the 'real world' of conflict and uncertainty, Mill's liberal idea of discovering truths through unhindered free debate becomes difficult, if not impossible, to sustain. Warburton's reminder that 'life isn't a seminar' serves as a prelude to the warning that words are more dangerous than Mill imagined.

In a world where governments and advocacy groups are continually organizing campaigns to save people from their bad habits, Mill's argument that individuals should not be compelled to refrain from harming themselves, only from injuring others, is also widely questioned. The harm principle is continually questioned and tested on the grounds that 'there are no actions solely affecting the agent; because all actions, in principle at least, have an effect on others'.[7] Robert Paul Wolff argues that a devout Calvinist or vegetarian might be 'harmed' because the 'very presence in his community of a Catholic or a meat-eater may cause him fully as much pain as a blow to the face or the theft of his purse'.[8] However, being affected is not the same as being harmed. Mill did not deny that presence of Catholics might distress devout Calvinists: as Beattie writes, 'Instead, he denied that such distress is a harm warranting government intervention or regulation'.[9]

Queries about the definition of harm raise questions about whether it touches on merely the physical domain, or whether it pertains to the domain of the mental and moral. Some question the possibility of drawing a 'clear distinction' between actions that cause harm and actions which merely provoke 'offence, disgust or disapproval'. Moreover, as Mendus asks, 'are actions which provoke offence, disgust or disapproval themselves harmful?'[10] In contemporary times the meaning of harm is continually contested on a wide variety of issues, such as pornography, abortion, school examination, advertising, or offensive speech. From time to time philosophers and legal scholars try to help resolve these disputes by attempting to provide a definition of the harm principle, but the meaning of harm is ultimately resolved through political debate and conflict.

Perceptions of harm, pain and suffering are mediated through cultural norms, and underwritten by a script that informs communities about their meaning. In this respect, twenty-first-century Western societies have a uniquely low threshold for experiencing harm: as discussed elsewhere, they are dominated by a culture of fear in which virtually every human experience comes with a health warning.[11] Hitherto taken-for-granted activities, such as sunbathing or eating meat, are now reinterpreted as risky. The increasing variety of physical harms has been supplemented by recently invented emotional ones, and society's therapeutic turn has led to a refocusing of the way harm is perceived. As a result it is now common to represent emotional injury to the individual as more damaging than physical injury. Expressions like 'scarred for life' or 'damaged for life' are said to be the harmful effects of the trauma that afflicts children, while adults are also instructed that emotional injury can cause lifelong harm.

The meaning of harm has always been subject to cultural and social variations. Practices that have been deemed harmful to the point of causing irreparable damage to body and soul, for example masturbation, are today praised as valid ways of expressing sexual desire. Similarly, today's pathologies – stress, low self-esteem, indeed most forms of psychological distress – were in the past perceived as existential problems rather than as serious medical harms. The diagnosis of a growing variety of psychological harms should be interpreted as an act of social construction, rather than the discovery of objective facts. Warburton states that 'many writers would today recognize that psychological harms can be as personally damaging as physical ones, so would be less inclined to focus solely on physical harms than was Mill'.[12] This statement means that today's definition of harm is influenced by a therapeutic sensibility that perceives emotions as constantly at risk from a variety of threats. This problematization of emotional life has widened the definition of harm to a historically unprecedented point.

Unlike physical harm, emotional harm is limited only by the imagination. Regardless of intent, a gesture or comment can be perceived in a way that causes emotional harm. According to child protection guidelines used in Britain, emotional abuse can refer to virtually every parental failing, from 'failure to meet a child's need for affection' to being so 'overprotective and possessive' that parents prevent their children from experiencing 'normal social contact or normal physical activity'.[13] Despite its nebulous character, in 2009 'more children were placed on the at-risk register for emotional harm than for sexual abuse or physical abuse'.[14] The expansion of the diagnosis of emotional harm is not confined to children: in a culture where individuals are incited to regard themselves as being at risk, relatively routine encounters are likely to be perceived as potentially damaging to the emotion. The term 'emotional bullying' widely used in the workplace is an example of the current trend towards the expansion and infantilization of harm. Contemporary cultural norms work to lower the threshold of acceptable distress, and encourage individuals to interpret unpleasant experiences as damaging to their health and emotions.

How people cope with painful encounters is strongly influenced by cultural and historical factors that shape the way we sense them. Such cultural factors may increase or reduce the ability of the individual to cope with adverse circumstances. The current tendency to problematize identity and emotion inexorably encourages people to perceive unpleasant encounters, disappointments and slights as harmful to their psyche. In relation to identity, it is argued that harm can be done simply by being neutral, and not appearing to offer respect and recognition. Even being ignored by colleagues and other people is represented as a variant of emotional abuse. At the very least, such experiences are held responsible for lowering people's self-esteem, which is conceived of as an invisible disease that undermines people's ability to control their lives. The constant problematization of human emotion inexorably leads to its recycling in a disease form. Once responses to adversity are culturally validated in a disease form they will, sooner or later, be experienced as harmful. Hence therapeutic culture fuels the expansion of the range of experiences that can be labelled as harmful.

The transformation of distress into a condition of emotional injury is now validated by the law. With the expansion of the meaning of harm, mental anguish and suffering have become legitimate claims for compensation. On both sides of the Atlantic the harms caused by psychological distress provide the ground for awards in a growing percentage of personal injury cases. Protecting people from the harms associated with psychological distress is also used to curb tolerance towards those whose words cause harm.

The expansion of the meaning of harm is directly proportional to the contraction of tolerance towards hurtful and offensive speech. As the number and variety of actions and behaviours which are deemed to harm people's psyche and dignity increases, so the territory on which tolerance is tolerated contracts. Harel has argued that 'an exploration of the proper boundaries of tolerance in modern society should be based on its impact on the well-being of individuals'.[15] But if people's well-being is so easily compromised by an ever-increasing variety of harms, the boundaries of tolerance will be drawn very narrowly. The all-too-frequent diagnosis of psychic injury legitimizes a very strict rationing of tolerance.

Calls for curbing free speech today are far less likely to be presented as a response to curbing subversion than in the past. Today the censor's eyes are directed at offensive material rather than subversion, and banning such material is invariably represented as essential for preventing the harm caused by psychic injury. For Harell it is the negative impact of hurtful speech on the 'psychological and physical well-being of racialized minorities' that constitutes the problem, as this harms the 'equal ability of people to enjoy the rights accorded to them as citizens'.[16] The link between speech and psychic harm often has an arbitrary and promiscuous character. Parekh explains that some targets of hate speech 'internalise their negative image and develop self-abasement and low self-esteem, or compensate for it by becoming aggressive and self-righteous'.

Others 'tend to avoid activities, occupations and careers where they fear hatred, cannot be sure of equal treatment and basic respect'. Parekh concedes that the harms caused are 'not easy to identify and measure' but is nonetheless confident that 'they can be profound and real'.[17]

Recent decades have seen a proliferation of psychological symptoms that are allegedly caused by offensive speech and behaviour. Matsuda writes that 'the negative effects of vicious hate propaganda have experienced psychological symptoms and emotional distress ranging from fear in the gut, rapid pulse rate and difficulty breathing, nightmares, post traumatic disorder, hypertension, psychosis and suicide'.[18] Others claim that hate speech produces physical symptoms that temporarily disable its targets. Numerous advocates of censorship adopt the rhetorical strategy of portraying offensive language as a threat akin to extreme forms of physical violence. Patricia William depicts racist communications as a form of 'spirit murder', while Matsuda interprets them as acts of 'psychic destruction'.[19] She describes 'assaultive speech' as composed of 'words that are used as weapons to ambush, terrorize, wound, humiliate, and degrade'.[20]

As Mill and other liberal thinkers have recognized, words have power. Indeed it was precisely because these thinkers understood the potential power of speech that they so vigorously took up the cause of the freedom to communicate. However, the recognition of the impact and influence of words is different to the current project of transforming it into a dangerous weapon. A verbal assault should not be confused with a physical one. When a bullet is fired by a gun, its harm to the person can be more or less interpreted as a direct consequence of the act of physical assault; there is no such direct relationship between targeting a person with an insult and the intensity of the hurt caused. An insult hurled at people in anger is mediated through a system of meaning, the psychological disposition of different individuals, and the context within which it occurs. Whether it wounds or merely irritates depends on the perceptions and subjectivity of those involved.

The social construction of the idiom of assaultive speech involves a fundamental reconceptualization of the working of language. At its worst it fetishizes words, reinventing them as objects that contain destructive properties in and of themselves. Historically, the fetishization of words emerged with ancient mystical and religious thought: according to numerous creation myths, saying the word could turn it into reality, while a spell or a curse could literally destroy lives. In ancient Egypt it was believed that the spoken word had a transformative impact on the world. In some religions, the word for God could not be said for fear of unleashing its wrath. These early fantasies of ancient superstition have now been recycled by opponents of free speech in the shape of psychic threats.

The fetishization of language has gained most traction around the issue of pornography. Since pornography self-consciously seeks to objectify sexual desire, it readily lends itself to the interpretation that it, itself, is an object of harm. In the 1980s leading feminist anti-pornography campaigners such as Catherine MacKinnon and Andrea Dworkin developed a thesis that interpreted pornography as a form of violence in itself. From this perspective, not only is the distinction between words and action lost, but the image itself is objectified as harm itself. Accordingly, pornography is not an image or a representation of sexual degradation, but an act. MacKinnon defines pornography as 'a form of forced sex' with the power to 'construct who that is'. As Rauch observes, what MacKinnon implies is 'not that pornography *causes* hurt, but that it is hurt' and that 'it is violence: specifically, it is *group* violence against women'.[21] The depiction of pornography as a harm has provided a paradigm for the objectification of speech in other domains of social experience. Through the amplification of the harmful properties of words and speech, language itself has can be represented as a form of toxin. From this perspective, the very act of communicating unpleasant ideas and words is portrayed as a manifestation of moral pollution. 'Often the hate speech is intended to be contagious – part of the desired effect is to encourage others to express similarly venomous views', warns Warburton.[22] Public speech acts are, of course, designed to 'encourage others'. But instead of countering a bad speech with a good one, the diagnosis of a contagious, venomous disease leads to the call for quarantine.

The diseasing of words is not confined to pornography or hate speech: any unpleasant communication can be interpreted as a health problem. 'We always knew that words could hurt our *feelings*, but it turns out that words have a profound effect on our *bodies* as well' claims 'life-coach' Linda Pucci in her discussion of 'toxic words'.[23] In recent decades, numerous advocacy organizations have embraced the fetishization of speech so that diverse forms of offensive and xenophobic speech are imagined, not just as harmful, but as actual harms. The cumulative effect of the transformation of words into metaphorical weapons is the erosion of the line dividing speech from action. Through medicalizing the effects of speech, wounded pride is diagnosed as comparable to, if not the equivalent of, a severed limb.

If speech can be inherently harmful, why not our thoughts?[24] And indeed since the invention of hate crimes, the legal distinction between what we think and what we do has become blurred. Questioning the freedom of belief is justified on the ground that a belief like hate leads to the expression of harmful words which serve as a prelude to psychic or physical violence. In such circumstances, even Locke's call for tolerating belief comes unstuck.

Towards therapeutic censorship

In the context of the expansion of the meaning of harm, words are frequently depicted as weapons that can damage their targets psychologically. Consequently, the right to free speech often competes with the 'right' not to be offended. From this perspective censorship is perceived not as a form of authoritarian intrusion, but as an enlightened measure designed to protect the vulnerable from pain. The idea that language offends is not new; but the notion that because offensive speech has such damaging consequences for people that it needs to be closely regulated represents a significant departure from the way it has been conceptualized in previous times.

Such an orientation has as its premise a radical redefinition of human subjectivity, which assumes that people lack the intellectual resources to deal with competing ideas. As we argue in the next chapter, present-day advocates of censoring speech imagine that the public lacks moral autonomy and needs to be protected from making the wrong choices in the marketplace of ideas. In such circumstances ideas can be very dangerous and their suppression represented as an act of public service. It is a sign of the times that acts of censorship are not interpreted as what they really are – the coercive regulation of everyday communication, and the repression and stigmatization of certain ideas. Instead, they are often represented as enlightened attempts to prevent offending people, or as a sensible way of minimizing conflict.

The advocacy of therapeutic censorship by social psychologists gained influence among American opinion-makers in the 1950s. Gordon Allport argued for the regulation of speech to free people from 'word fetishism', in order to 'liberate a person from ethnic or political prejudice'. He concluded that 'any program for the reduction of prejudice must include a large measure of semantic therapy'.[25] Since the 1950s, Allport's advocacy of semantic therapy has been adopted by numerous institutions and provides the rationale for the current proliferation of speech codes.

In controversies that surround tolerance, it is frequently suggested that it is morally legitimate to curb speech that is offensive or that insults an individual or a group. Time and again there are calls to punish people for disrespecting a culture, insulting a group, or offending an individual. What is overlooked is that freedom of speech requires the expression of opinions which some deem insulting and hurtful. Just as Justice Oliver Wendell Holmes argued is his widely cited comment, 'every idea is an incitement', today he would be more likely to insist that 'every idea is offensive'. 'If liberty means anything', argued George Orwell, 'it means the right to tell people what they do not want to hear'. Unfortunately, in the current therapeutic climate telling people what they do not want to hear is readily diagnosed as insulting, disrespectful, a wound to their identity, and a form of psychological harm.

The emphasis that critics of tolerance of free speech place on offensive words is underpinned by the project of diseasing language. Since to offend is to cause psychological damage, the regulation of language is implicitly interpreted as a service for the maintenance of public health. Offensive speech becomes stigmatized as an immoral act rather than a form of speech that can or ought to be countered by logical argument. In this way the diseasing of offensive words allows acts of censorship to assume a benevolent and therapeutic form, as cures to the disease. This is what Matsuda means when she writes that 'as we learn more about the compulsive/psychosocial aspects of racism, we may come to see how allowing the racist speaker to fall into an accelerating upward spiral or racist behaviour is akin to letting a disease go untreated'.[26] The diagnosis of offensive speech as a disease provides a rationale for depicting it as the words of a mentally imbalanced person that need not be taken seriously. A very similar diagnosis was used in the old Soviet Union, where dissident voices were sometimes despatched to the mental asylum.

In previous times intolerance towards people's beliefs and speech was directed at heretical doctrines or subversive ideologies. Governments argued that unregulated speech might incite violence and disorder. Outwardly, laws directed towards restraining the freedom of speech in Britain are still defended on the grounds that they help prevent outbreaks of violence. But a careful reading of laws like the Incitement to Religious Hatred Act indicates that such legislation is motivated by the imperative of protecting the feelings of those who may feel aggrieved by insults to their religion. Since the 1980s the cause of suppressing speech or images that could cause offence has acquired the status of a moral crusade. All it took was for a group of Sikhs to complain that a play in Birmingham offended their culture for government ministers to condone its shutting down.

With the shift from the banning of the subversive to the suppression of the offensive, there has been an important change in the workings of censorship. Back in Roman times two magistrates or 'censors' were charged not only with counting the population but also with the supervision of public morals. Although in the nineteenth and twentieth centuries censorship was frequently driven by a political imperative, its aim remained essentially the policing of moral behaviour. Twenty-first-century censorship continues this tradition of moral enterprise, but often in a therapeutic form. It is no longer simply the project of state or religious authorities: advocacy groups, educators, media organizations and professionals are actively engaged in rhetorical crusades to ban certain words, customs and practices. Since the beginning of modern times there has never been an era where language is as carefully policed by both private and public institutions as it is today. Campaigning groups carefully review newspapers, reports and television programmes for offensive words, while speech codes that specify words that must not be used and helpfully provide 'appropriate' alternative expressions have become institutionalized in public and private institutions. They have constructed a veritable lexicon of single-letter initial words like N word, B word, F word and R word. There are even advocacy organizations whose entire existence is devoted to abolishing a word altogether.[27]

In its therapeutic form, censorship is often misinterpreted as a progressive initiative to prevent people from suffering psychological harm. Therapeutic censorship does not appear as the suppression of freedom, but as an exercise in sensitive behaviour management. One regrettable consequence of the belief that intolerance towards harmful speech is necessary to protect minorities and the vulnerable is that movements that have traditionally supported free speech have switched sides. Historically, it was left-wing radicals and progressives who were the most consistent supporters of tolerance and the freedom of speech, but in recent times the left's embrace of the politics of recognition means that this constituency can no longer be counted upon to advocate tolerance. Indeed it can be argued that if anything, those who identify themselves as left wing are likely to be more censorious than their counterparts on the right. This development is particularly striking in the birthplace of identity politics, the United States. This comment, by free speech advocate Steven Gey, is apposite:

> It is an unfortunate sign of our ambiguous times that the First Amendment's free speech protection no longer commands universal support among progressive constitutional scholars and legal activists. The political and legal circles that only a decade ago could be counted on to defend First Amendment values are now increasingly willing to qualify their support for free speech, if not to abandon the cause altogether.[28]

In the twenty-first century there is no significant intellectually or politically discernible constituency that is genuinely committed to the principle of tolerance and the freedom of speech.

There was a time when those who called themselves radical or progressive struggled for the realization of the right to freedom of speech. These days, so-called progressives are far more likely to demonstrate *against* the right of people that they don't like to speak openly. It is now an article of faith on campuses that speakers who espouse allegedly racist, misogynist or homophobic views should not be allowed to speak. Banning Zionist speakers is also justified as a blow for progressive politics. The cult of intolerance on campuses indicates that academia is no longer a haven for critical thinking and free speech. As Wendy Kaminer, the American civil liberties activist, observes:

> One of the saddest trends among people who consider themselves liberal or progressive over the past 10 or 15 years has been this increased intolerance of free speech, and this notion

that there is some right, some civil right, not to be offended, which trumps somebody else's right to speak in a way that you find offensive. It is like a disease, an infection, that has taken hold on the left. It is an incredibly regressive notion.[29]

The desire to protect individuals from offence is underwritten by a powerful new cultural script. This means that, today, there is only a very feeble cultural affirmation for freedom of speech. Indeed, one often gets the impression that academics and public figures are more interested in criticizing the ideal of free speech than they are in upholding it. Many thinkers seem unperturbed by the role of the state in policing speech. Thus the original impetus behind the demand for free speech, which was based on a fear of the power of the state to censor and persecute people for their beliefs and words, is dismissed as an historical footnote.

Those who are concerned about state intervention into public debate are looked upon as having an old-fashioned and irrelevant obsession. One critic notes that 'free speech advocacy is steeped in the historical context' and that therefore the First Amendment is 'a direct expression' of the historic 'fear of state power'. His implicit conclusion is that it is therefore no big deal and writes, with apparent puzzlement, that for 'First Amendment absolutists, state power is inherently suspect'.[30]

The advocacy of free speech was historically an integral part of the movement for democratization, and for creating the conditions where the poor and dispossessed could find their voice. With the diseasing of speech the liberal and democratic interpretation of free speech is challenged by influential intellectual and political forces who take the view that, on balance, tolerance needs to be rationed. Instead of regarding the state regulation of speech as a threat to civil liberties, these thinkers embrace it as an essential instrument for inoculating society from linguistic harm.

Some self-identified progressive thinkers and activists associate free speech with elite privilege, presenting it as something that protects the status of the powerful and negates the views or feelings of the oppressed and vulnerable. This radical reinterpretation of the role of free speech is paralleled by a fundamental redefinition of what constitutes the problem: for today's critics of free speech, the locus of the problem is not the state but the offensive words and behaviour of individuals. They focus their concern on individual forms of speech that wound those without power, overlooking the institutional and cultural influences on public debate and perceiving the task of protecting the individual from psychological pain as logically prior to upholding the right to free speech.

Free speech is thus treated as a risk factor that needs to be assessed in relation to the potential harm that it can cause the individual. One advocate of rationing tolerance states that he is concerned about the 'risks the right of free speech entails for socially disadvantaged individuals within the community of enfranchised speakers'.[31] Such pronouncements appear entirely indifferent to the risks entailed by the suppression of the right to free communication.

From this warped perspective, state censorship has an actively positive role to play. Through enforcing laws that apparently protect people from hate and hurt, the therapeutic censorship of the state is often depicted as an act of championing the powerless. All too often in public debates, the risk of free speech appears as a greater threat than the risk of not tolerating it.

The cultivation of vulnerability

Of course tolerance is risky. Once conventional restraints to belief, opinion and speech are removed, it becomes difficult to predict the future course of public life. The freedom to speak and to pursue knowledge has a habit of going off in unexpected directions. One reason why communities find it uncomfortable to be entirely open to freedom is because they often yearn for the taken-for-granted and predictable patterns of previous times.

However, a positive orientation towards risk-taking has always been a hallmark of societies that took liberty seriously. It was in ancient Athens, the cradle of democracy, that risk-taking first acquired a positive cultural valuation, with risk-taking and freedom regarded as mutually reinforcing values.[32] A similar trend is discernible in the life of the Italian city states during the Renaissance, where the development of early ideas about liberty was paralleled by a disposition towards exploration. To this day, the First Amendment to the US Constitution affords greater protection to the freedom of speech than is available in Europe, and the widening of the interpretation of the First Amendment was inextricably bound up with a robust attitude towards risk-taking.

Locke took a tremendous risk when he called for the tolerance of dissident religious sects, and the gradual expansion of toleration in liberal democracies is indicative of these societies' confidence. As Fletcher points out, 'the more tolerant we are of risks, the less likely we are to intervene'.[33] A society that is confident about its capacity to engage with uncertainty is likely to trust in its citizens' ability to use their freedoms in a responsible manner. Justice Louis Brandeis was clearly cognizant of people's fears about speech-induced harms, but he took the view that censorship was not the answer:

Those who won our independence . . . recognized the risks to which all human institutions are subject. But they knew that . . . it is hazardous to discourage thought, hope and imagination; that fear breeds repression; that repression breeds hate, that hate menaces stable governments; that the path of safety lies in the opportunity to discuss freely supposed grievances and proposed remedies . . . Fear of serious injury cannot alone justify suppression of free speech.[34]

The Supreme Court jurist Oliver Wendell Holmes, who played a crucial role in upholding a progressive interpretation of the First Amendment, argued that the US Constitution obliged citizens to an 'experiment' based on the premise that 'the best test of truth is the power of the thought to get itself accepted in the competition of the market'.[35] Holmes' analogy of an experiment captures open-ended trajectory of the pursuit of freedom. When a society discourages people from taking risks, risk-taking becomes equated with irresponsible behaviour and precaution is turned into a virtue. Such a society is likely to be uncomfortable with the virtue of tolerance and will attempt to foster a climate of conformist behaviour.

Present-day Western societies have become characteristically risk averse and, as a result, values that are usually associated with openness towards new experience have become less and less influential. In everyday usage the words 'experiment' and 'experimentation' have acquired negative, if not sinister, connotations. The idea of risk itself has been reinterpreted and is regularly used as a substitute for terms such as 'danger' or 'peril', while risky behaviour is described by public health officials as acts of irresponsibility. Risk aversion has encouraged the massive extension of the regulation of public and private life, as in the name of health and safety concerns every domain of human experience has become subject to micro-management. In such circumstances it is not surprising that the regulation of speech and communication is interpreted as a sensible response to the management of risk.

There are many drivers of intolerance and risk. One of the significant influences is the alarmist sensibility that disposes society towards the inflation of harm.[36] This does not simply reflect a response to the problems facing people, but a statement about people. The flip side of the expansion of the meaning of harm is the flourishing belief that humanity is defined by its powerlessness and vulnerability. The assumption that people lack the resilience to deal with hurtful language offers a dreary and pessimistic account of personhood, as critics of free speech often communicate the belief that the recipients of hurtful or insulting speech are too powerless to respond effectively.

Today's unprecedented sensitivity to people's vulnerability to emotional harm is underwritten by a distinct, diminished outlook on personhood, fuelled by a cultural code about the workings of human subjectivity. Every culture provides a set of ideas and beliefs about the nature of human beings; our ideas about what we can expect from one another, how we handle uncertainty and change, how we deal with adversity and pain, and how we respond to words are underpinned by the particular account that a culture offers about the human potential. As I argue elsewhere, the defining feature of the version of personhood offered by twenty-first-century Western society is its vulnerability.[37] Although society rhetorically upholds the ideals of self-determination and autonomy, the values associated with them are overridden by a message that stresses the quality of human frailty.

The diseasing of language is in part justified by the allegation that words cause emotional harm. However, this allegation is coupled with the thesis that some people are particularly vulnerable to the pain inflicted by such harm. Orville Lee uses the metaphor of 'linguistic vulnerability' to support his claim that it is people's position of powerlessness that renders them helpless to deal with some of the effects of speech, writing that 'the subject's vulnerability to the force of words' exists *'prior* to the institutional configuration of speakers and linguistic meanings'.[38] Lee is not closed to the possibility that 'linguistic vulnerability' may coexist with the possibility of people using speech to their advantage, while others adopt a one-sidedly fatalistic interpretation of the workings of diminished subjectivity. Matsuda and her co-thinkers insist that no matter how much people struggle to resist hate propaganda, the effect of this assault is devastating.[39]

The modern era has always contained political currents that query people's capacity to deliberate and engage in public debate. In the nineteenth century it was feared that obscenity laws were essential to protect people whose minds were vulnerable to immoral influences.[40] However, such pessimistic accounts of people's capacity to participate in public life as valuable citizens were continually contested by supporters of democracy and freedom, and despite periodic setbacks the liberal democratic ideal of free debate and tolerance possessed significant authority over public life. This sentiment was summed up in Hans Kelsen's well-known 1940s formulation of democracy:

> The will of the community, in a democracy, is always created through a running discussion between majority and minority, through free consideration of arguments for and against a certain regulation of a subject matter. This discussion takes place not only in parliament, but also, and foremost, at political

meetings, in newspapers, books, and other vehicles of public opinion. A democracy without public opinion is a contradiction in terms . . . public opinion can arise only where the intellectual freedom, freedom of speech and press and religion, are guaranteed.[41]

The freedoms upheld by Kelsen are now often treated as distinctly old-fashioned, mixed blessings that cause pain to some. Many question the authority of unquestioned freedom because they feel that a significant section of society lacks the emotional and psychological strengths and skills to cope with the pressure of public life. So Galeotti's advocacy of censorship is motivated by her belief that unless people are protected from the psychological and existential harm caused by hurtful speech, they will suffer. She writes of the 'feeling of shame, humiliation, and self-hatred' of people whose identity is not validated, and insists that this 'prevents people from developing an adequate level of self-respect and self-esteem, both of which are necessary, for developing and for making it heard, as well as for enjoying rights and for participating fully in the polity'.[42]

A close reading of this diagnosis of the public indicates that it is not so much the harm of speech that motivates those who reject tolerance: rather, it is a lack of confidence in ordinary people's ability to assume the role of mature citizens. If people genuinely suffer from the kind of psychological deficit that prevents them from 'participating fully in the polity', protecting them from offensive words and other confusing communications becomes a public duty.

Be warned, however: the rationing of tolerance does not confine itself to the censorship of outrageous words. Eventually it will adopt the conviction that people need not only protection from others' speech and behaviour but also from themselves. As

I argue in the next chapter, the rejection of tolerance towards the freedom of speech is profoundly motivated by a lack of respect for individual autonomy.

Notes

1 Mill (2008), p. 14.
2 Beattie (2004), p. 385.
3 Edwards (1988), p. 89.
4 Beattie (2004), p. 380.
5 John Gray's introduction to Mill (2008), p. xviii.
6 Warburton (2009), p. 31.
7 Beattie (2004), p. 379.
8 Cited by Beattie (2004), p. 379.
9 Beattie (2004), p. 380.
10 Mendus (1989), pp. 121, 123.
11 See Furedi (2006).
12 Warburton (2009), p. 31.
13 Cited in Furedi (2004b).
14 Cavendish (2010).
15 Harel, A. (1996), p. 114.
16 Harell (2010), p. 410.
17 Parekh (2006), p. 218.
18 Matsuda et al. (1993), p. 6.
19 Matsuda et al. (1993), p. 6.
20 Matsuda et al. (1993), p. 1.
21 Rauch (1993), pp. 16 and 17.
22 Warburton (2009), p. 56.
23 See Pucci (n.d.).
24 For a discussion of the recently invented hate crime against religion see 'Atkinson's religious hate worry', BBC News, 7 December 2004: http://news.bbc.co.uk/1/hi/uk_politics/4073997.stm (accessed 17 February 2011).
25 Allport (1954), p. 46.
26 Matsuda cited in Gey (1996), p. 203.

27 For example, the crusade to abolish the R word; see www.r-word. org.
28 Gey (1996), p. 193.
29 Cited by O'Neill (2006).
30 Lee (2001), p. 850.
31 Lee (2001), p. 849.
32 For an interesting exploration of this point, see Gouldner (1965).
33 Fletcher (1996), p. 158.
34 Cited in Strossen (1996), pp. 457–8.
35 Cited in Dworkin (1996), p. 199.
36 On this trend see Furedi (2006).
37 See Furedi (2004a), chapter 5.
38 Lee (2001), p. 864
39 See Matsuda et al. (1993), p. 25.
40 See Gey (1996) for a discussion of this point.
41 Cited in Urbinati (2002), p. 157.
42 Galeotti (2002), p. 9.

6

The Loss of Respect for Moral Independence

Government rulings and unofficial opinions about which views and practices should be tolerated and which should be censored are informed by prior assumptions about the workings of personhood. All debates on tolerance and freedom of speech make implicit assumptions about people's capacity to use their rights responsibly. Historically, censors took it for granted that people did not possess the capacities necessary to avoid being corrupted by immoral and dangerous ideas, and the belief that people are easily swayed by demagogues continues to motivate calls ban offensive words and images.

However, the target of censorship has changed. Yesterday's censors sought to protect people from various forms of moral degradation that were presumed to occur after exposure to the ideas of religious heretics, witches, freethinkers and libertines; today, the targets are more diffuse and can vary from pornography to hate speech to the temptations transmitted through commercial advertising. Censors do not demand that the transgressor ought to be burned at the stake: they call for banning an advertisement, silencing someone who makes offensive remarks, or punishing a so-called hate crime.

Contemporary censorship assumes that people lack the

moral antidote to resist being infected by the virus of offensive speech and images. It presupposes that pornography leads men to commit sexual violence against women or that hate speech serves as the catalyst for acts of aggression. It is convinced that people are so suggestible that they passively, even unwittingly, act on whatever idea or image is communicated to them. Twenty-first-century intolerance justifies its censorious practices on the grounds that it protects people from themselves as well as from the powerful influences that mislead or seduce them.

Widespread scepticism about people's capacity to respond to dangerous ideas with maturity indicates that society finds it difficult to take seriously the value of moral autonomy. Autonomy is an attribute of a person who engages with the world as an active, reasoning and conscious individual. The etymology of this word: *autos* (self) and *nomos* (rule or law) conveys the meaning of self-rule. The term was first used in the Greek city-states: according to one account, a 'city has *autonomia* when its citizens make their own laws, as opposed to being under the control of some conquering power'.[1]

An autonomous person is presumed to possess moral independence – in other words to act with moral responsibility. Through the exercise of autonomy people can develop their personality through assuming responsibility for their life. The cultivation of moral independence requires that people are free to deliberate and come to their own conclusions about the views and opinions they hear. As Ronald Dworkin explains:

> Government insults its citizens, and denies their moral responsibility, when it decrees that they cannot be trusted to hear opinions that might persuade them to dangerous or offensive convictions. We retain our dignity, as individual, only by

insisting that no one – no official and no majority – has the right to withhold an opinion from us on the ground that we are not fit to hear and consider it.[2]

Through reflecting freely on opinions and deciding for ourselves what is good and bad, we learn to behave as responsible and independent citizens. In the course of such deliberations, people not only forge their own opinions but also influence the views of others. The exercise of moral responsibility thus possesses an active dimension of seeking to communicate one's views to fellow citizens.

The exercise of moral autonomy requires that people are able to be themselves, act in accordance with their inclinations and tastes, and feel free to adopt a lifestyle that allows them to express their personality. As Dworkin states, 'citizens have as much right to contribute to the formation of the moral or aesthetic climate as they do to participate in politics'.[3] Hence, in order to respect people's moral autonomy, tolerance towards social attitudes is as necessary as tolerance towards beliefs and opinions. As Raz writes, 'autonomy requires that many morally acceptable, though incompatible, forms of life be available to a person'.[4]

The valuation of autonomy should not be interpreted to mean a naive populist belief in the capacity of the public to do no wrong. Millions of people continue to be prey to conspiracy theories, prejudices and irrational influences. Even at the best of times, individual autonomy is an ideal that can be realized inconsistently. People live in a world not of their own making and in circumstances that often elude their aspiration to determine their affairs. The exercise of autonomy has always come up against external constraints – natural obstacles, economic exigencies, wars and conflict, and social dislocation. Today it also faces a cultural climate that is deeply suspicious of the aspiration for autonomous behaviour.

The recognition that autonomy is morally valuable and that attempts by people to make their own decision should be respected does not mean that people always make the right choices for themselves. Nor should an ideal be confused with the attempt to realize it: formidable obstacles always stand in the way of individuals who wish to be authors of their own lives. But the difficulties that stand in the way of the realization of personal autonomy should not be interpreted as representing the negation of this ideal: people possess the potential for the exercise of moral independence. As with all freedoms, how autonomy is exercised and whether its potential is realized depends on specific circumstances. As Dworkin points out, there is a clear distinction to be made between the 'general point or value of autonomy and its consequences for a particular person on a particular occasion'.[5] It is precisely because autonomy is difficult to realize that there is such a great need for tolerance: as Raz states, a 'powerful argument in favour of toleration is derivable from the value of personal autonomy'.[6] Unfortunately, Western society has drawn the opposite conclusion, and in line with its loss of valuation for moral independence, it does not regard tolerance as a value in its own right.

Popular culture continually signals suspicion towards the exercise of human agency. In numerous accounts, the ideal of individual autonomy is dismissed as an illusion fostered by apologists for the free market. It is argued that in a society dominated by the media, big corporations, and the forces unleashed by globalization, individuals lack the capacity for autonomous action. Often people are portrayed as unwitting victims of the media, powerless to resist its subliminal messages – so they are kindly offered therapeutic censorship. Unfortunately, the transmission of this message by well-meaning educators, intellectuals and policymakers has the effect of discouraging people from discovering their own road to moral independence.

Loss of respect for moral independence

Modern society has never been able to uphold the idea of moral independence consistently. On occasions, even Mill had his doubts. His lack of faith in parents' ability to educate their children exposed such reservations about moral autonomy, which is why he linked his call for compulsory schooling to his mistrust of parental competence. Mill regarded state-sponsored formal education as possessing the capacity to free children from the 'uncultivated' influence of their parents, asserting that since 'the uncultivated cannot be competent judges of cultivation' they needed the support of enlightened educators to socialize their children.[7] Mill made an implicit distinction between the 'cultivated' and the 'uncultivated' in relation to the possession of the moral capacity to educate the younger generation. Today, however, the moral capacity of people to discriminate, evaluate and reflect is questioned far more systematically.

The idea of linguistic vulnerability discussed in the previous chapter is linked to an interpretation of human personality that assumes that powerlessness and immaturity are its dominant features. The term 'vulnerability' is habitually used as if it is a permanent feature of a person's biography, presented and experienced as a natural state of being that shapes human response. It is a label that is inscribed on entire groups in society, which is why it has become so common to use the recently constructed concept of 'vulnerable groups'. Moreover, this state of vulnerability is presented as an intrinsic, essential attribute of the group, something that is fundamental to the individuals' identities and personhoods.

Almost all therapeutic censorship-led initiatives predicate their action on the belief that people are too vulnerable to handle their exposure to dangerous words. Once the assumption that people are potentially morally autonomous is displaced by the conviction that they are vulnerable and lacking in the capacity to make choices, the case for tolerance and the freedom of speech is significantly undermined. From this standpoint it is difficult to avoid the conclusion that people are unlikely to have the independence to develop ideas consistent with their self-interest.

People getting their 'fundamental interests wrong is what American political life is all about', notes Thomas Frank in his bestseller *What's the Matter with America?* Otherwise, Frank argues, how could they possibly vote for the Republicans?[8] Such patronizing assumptions about the mental capacities of ordinary folk are widespread in contemporary political discourse. The belief that people are too immature to grasp the complexities of public life was widely expressed during the heated exchanges around the EU constitution: Margot Wallström, the EU's former vice president, commented on her blog that the constitution is a 'complex issue to vote on' which can confuse many citizens, who may 'use a referendum to answer a question that was not put to them'.[9] Whatever the rights and wrongs of the populist rejection of the EU treaty, the manner in which the 'No' campaign was disparaged by professional politicians betrayed a powerful temper of intolerance towards an allegedly ignorant electorate.

Today's political elite expresses its disappointment with a public it does not understand through disparaging the electorate. In the US, this sentiment has been systematically articulated by Democratic Party activists, who could not quite grasp why many blue-collar workers voted for George Bush. According to George Lakoff, one of the most influential thinkers influencing the liberal wing of the Democrats, 'people do not necessarily vote in their self interest'.[10] That is Lakoff's indirect way of saying that people lack capacity for exercising moral independence.

Political elites have always tended to be anxious about public opinion, which is invariably treated as a 'problem'. The American commentator Walter Lippman's 1922 study, *Public Opinion*, provides the classic statement, warning that the proportion of the electorate that is 'absolutely illiterate' is much larger than we suspect and that these people who are 'mentally children or barbarians' are natural targets of manipulators.[11] The tendency to stigmatize populist politics as a symptom of psychological disorder and irrationalism has a long history. In his important study *The Populist Persuasion*, Michael Kazin notes that in the United States during the Cold War, populism became the 'great fear of liberal intellectuals', who blamed mass democracy and an 'authoritarian' and 'irrational' working class for being easily swayed by the demagogy of McCarthyism.[12] Classical allusions about fiery orators and mob rule call into question the virtue of free speech. It was in such circumstances that Allport developed his idea of semantic therapy.

In their role of the manipulated or potentially manipulated individuals, people can no longer be trusted to behave as responsible citizens. In such circumstances public life ceases to be a space where a clash of competing viewpoint helps to clarify the truth. The liberal conviction that a contest of conflicting ideas is likely to facilitate the development of knowledge is called into question by a very busy cohort of therapeutic censors. The model of the public as a collection of gullible, suggestible, easily manipulated and immature people is particularly influential among supporters of the project of regulating commercial advertising. Arguments that are used to justify the censorship or regulation of advertising for children are recycled to cover the gullible grown-up, who is supposedly no less prey to the seductive powers of commercials. But if adults need to be protected from being brainwashed by crafty advertisers, why not from individuals and organizations attempting to sell their dangerous ideas? Imperceptibly, the model of child protection for insulating children from misleading commercials has been extended to cover their elders. Therapeutic censorship both patronizes and infantilizes people and insists that it plays an essential role helping individuals to make the 'right choices'.

From the standpoint of democracy, free speech is valued because citizens benefit from being exposed to a wide range of competing opinions. It is by participating in such debates that a democratic community is established. Through speaking and evaluating other people's opinions, people learn to cultivate their capacity for critical engagement and cease to be passive recipients of handed-down dogma. Once people's capacity for moral independence is called into question, so is the authority of free speech. Crusaders advocating speech codes and laws to suppress offensive statements and attitudes often transmit a sense of contempt towards the authority of free speech: it is with more than a hint of self-righteousness that Richard Delgado states, 'the old formalist view of speech as a near-perfect instrument for testing ideas and promoting social progress is passing into history'.[13] The implication of Delgado's statement is that free speech is a myth and that in an unequal society the idea of a genuine open debate is an illusion. This cynical appraisal of the role of free speech is presented as an argument for the legitimation of its regulation. The principal premise of the case for the devaluation of the freedom of speech is the supposition that people lack the intellectual or moral independence to evaluate critically the views to which they are exposed. As Gey points out, what 'most offends critical race theorists' is the 'presumption that the intellectual "consumers" in the market place are free actors, capable of intelligently and fairly considering competing political ideas, policy proposals and value systems before forming conclusions of their own about the direction in which the country and its government should move'. This cynicism about people's potential to make free and intelligent choices is founded on the belief that people are not genuinely free to choose because 'the "consumers" in the market place of ideas are so infused with the received values of a corrupt system that they cannot possibly exercise independent judgment'.[14] In this model, mental enslavement trumps the capacity for autonomy. The inference conveyed by this pessimistic assessment of people's mental capacities is that since citizens cannot exercise independent judgement, they require someone else to do it for them. Although the paternalistic implications of this conclusion are rarely made explicit, they have become a premise of official thinking.

The absence of independent judgement is associated with the moral status assigned to children. Once adults are diagnosed as lacking the capacity to exercise independent judgement, they become infantilized. Even the most committed supporters of liberty, such as Mill, were unambiguously clear that the right to the exercise of freedom applied only to adults 'in the maturity of their faculties', and that those who lacked the capacity for moral independence could not be expected to use their freedom responsibly. Society no longer takes it for granted that adults possess 'the maturity of their faculties', and it is widely argued that people need not only to be protected from harmful ideas – they sometimes need to be coerced to adopt forms of behaviour for their own good.

The paternalistic impulse-driving therapeutic censorship is wedded to the conviction that the very attempt to exercise autonomy is an act of self-deception. People are presumed to be so strongly under the influence of irrational sentiments and opinions that they are virtual prisoners of prejudice and consumerist ideas. The American Psychiatric Association has identified a pathological condition called oniomania, otherwise known as compulsive shopping, in which, according to one account, people 'find their shopping is out of control', 'they buy more than they need' and are in the 'grip of a collective psychological disorder'.[15] The presumption that powerful messages from advertisers directly lead to compulsive shopping now extends to other forms of communications, inviting government and non-governmental agencies to intervene to protect people. In this way, the metaphor of compulsive behaviour and addiction invites society to call into question individual agency and capacity for self-determination.

Intolerance of private preference

The loss of respect accorded to moral independence is rarely explicitly justified or codified into a philosophical doctrine. Indeed public figures and opinion-makers continually uphold the ideal of personal responsibility. Prominent celebrities and icons of popular culture regularly advise their audience to 'do their own thing' and stress the importance of respecting other people, while therapists and self-help gurus deify the 'inner self' and the goals of self-realization and self-actualization. But this celebration of the self should not be confused with an affirmation of autonomy. The very exhortation to take responsibility for the care of the self coexists with a health warning about human vulnerability and powerlessness.

As in the past, contemporary culture sends out contradictory messages about the values it upholds. It continues to praise individual responsibility, individual initiative and independence, at the same time not quite believing that the majority of people possess the capacity for rational responsible behaviour. Since the turn of the twenty-first century, the capacity for moral independence has been queried by influential intellectual currents, and as a result governments unapologetically promote policies that disregard the private preference of individuals. A new ethos of intolerance towards the choices that people wish to make about how to conduct their lives is closely linked to the downgrading of the value of moral autonomy.

That people often make choices that are irrational and which they regret is no secret. People often discover that they have been a poor judge of character, too hasty in their rejection of what turned out to be sound advice, or that their behaviour resulted in negative consequences for their family and for themselves. However, advocates of liberty argue that people can profit from their mistakes, and that having to learn to live with the consequences of their actions raises the potential for people to become more mature and independent. A belief in freedom involves a preparedness to take a risk and allow people to develop through the process of self-determination.

In line with society's estrangement from risk-taking, an influential body of opinion believes that it is not right to allow people the freedom to experiment and make the 'wrong choices'. The recognition that people can, and often do, behave irrationally is frequently represented as an argument for regulating people's lifestyles. The UK's Royal Society of Art (RSA) has launched a project to promote policies that help people make the right choices, since apparently 'much of decision-making stems from "irrational" emotions and "gut instincts" rather than rational self-conscious deliberation'. The RSA's diagnosis of human irrationality serves as a warrant for assuming authority for directing people's lives. Given that individual freedom still enjoys a degree of public valuation, the RSA is hesitant about spelling out the coercive implications of its diagnosis, stating that 'wherever possible policy should not take away the free choice of individuals'.[16] Yet the term 'wherever possible' indicates a less-than-wholehearted commitment to free choice. It signifies that freedom is no longer perceived as a principle that is good in itself, and warns that where it isn't, the use of pressure is a legitimate policy option.

Arguments about the necessity of protecting people from themselves were traditionally conveyed on religious or philosophical grounds. Today the traditional categories of sinners and the morally inferior have been displaced by jargon drawn from behavioural economics, evolutionary psychology, and neuroscience. The resources of these disciplines have been mobilized effectively to discredit the idea of moral autonomy. But essentially what has changed is the rhetoric. Instead of making a statement on the status of human beings based on religious doctrine and moral categories, the RSA uses the language 'research shows', arguing that 'new research in neuroscience, behavioural economics and social psychology' is casting doubt on the idea that human behaviour is always rational and driven essentially by self-interest'.[17] During the past decade, the refrain 'new research shows' has been continually used to highlight the discovery that people are not always rational, and to demand policies that attempt to coerce people into desisting from acting in accordance with their beliefs or inclinations.

In the United States, advocates of civic republicanism claim that it is the role of government to promote what they call 'civic virtues'. Civic republicanism is uncomfortable with manifestations of populist democracy and looks to enlightened political leaders and experts to guide citizens in the desired direction. Harvard law professor Cass Sunstein, one of the principal proponents of civic republicanism, lacks the tolerance necessary for allowing civic virtues to emerge from a public contest of competing values, taking the view that it is government's role to 'instil the principles of virtue' in individual citizens.[18] That is why Sunstein believes that 'a democratic government should sometimes take private preferences as an object of regulation and control'.[19] Once private preference becomes a legitimate target of government control, it follows that there will be little tolerance towards behaviour deemed irrational or incorrect. Consequently, Sunstein is prepared to prohibit 'anti-social' speech such as pornography or hate speech, as well as discouraging people from consuming trashy entertainment formats.[20]

Sunstein's argument for a paternalistic form of governance has as its basis the belief that, left to their own devices, people make choices that are bad for them and for society. He contends that people do not tend to act in accordance with their self-interest, and that government therefore needs to step in. As Gey points out, what Sunstein wants is that 'government should be given the authority both to sort out the "actual" from the merely "subjectively perceived" individual preferences and to correct for "bad" social conditioning by creating an elaborate system of social controls and value instructions intended to produce individuals imbued with a range of government-dictated "actual" preferences'.[21] In previous times, this approach to policymaking was called social engineering; Sunstein prefers the label of 'libertarian paternalism'.

Sunstein's call to use state intervention to regulate private preference is motivated by his conviction that enlightened polices formulated by experts could influence people to make the kind of positive choices that benefit society as a whole. Ironically, he seems unaware of the contradictions between government intrusion into the domain of private choice and the workings of a democratic society. Typically, he applauds dissent but only so long as it is constructive: '[s]ometimes dissenters lead people in bad directions', he warns. Of course dissenting views can confuse and disorient people; but tolerance of dissent is not predicated on the guarantee that critics are always right. As Mill and other liberals noted, even dissent that is totally erroneous can be valuable for assisting the process of intellectual clarification. However, once people are perceived as likely to be irrational about making the 'right' choices, dissent becomes a risky luxury. Sunstein echoes this sentiment when he states that 'when conformists are doing the right thing, there is far less need for dissent': but who gets to decide what is the 'right thing'? Certainly not the people. Sustein refers to the climate change debate as an example of unhelpful dissent: 'If scientists have reached the correct conclusions about global warming', he writes, 'pseudo-scientists do us no favors in pushing nutty theories of their own'.[22]

Since the 1980s, when Sunstein first demanded that the private preference should be subject to government management, the arguments for controlling individual behaviour have gained significant academic legitimacy. Ideas developed in the disciplines of evolutionary psychology and behavioural economics have been deployed to develop his ideas further into the doctrine of *Nudge*.[23] These disciplines have gained considerable influence, in part because they appear to provide scientific justification for the current mood of scepticism about the exercise of human subjectivity. As Alan Wolfe explains, there has been widespread acclaim for the ideas 'associated with evolutionary psychology and behavioural economics, both of which deny the key liberal idea that human beings are free to live their lives in ways they collectively decide for themselves'.[24] The arguments put forward by Sunstein and his associates are important because they provide a coherent intellectual rationale for minimizing the risks attached to the free pursuit of private preference at a time when political elites feel deeply uncomfortable from engaging with uncertainty.

During the past decade, governments of all complexions have embraced one or another version of Sunstein's doctrines. President Obama appointed Sunstein as administrator of the White House's Office of Information and Regulatory Affairs, while in Britain both the New Labour government and the subsequent Conservative-Liberal Democrat coalition government have embraced the argument that it is the role of government to inculcate citizens with the correct virtues in order to influence their personal behaviour. These ideas, summarized in Sunstein and Thaler's bestselling book *Nudge*, can be interpreted as an eloquent statement of the traditional paternalistic sentiment 'we know better than you what's good for you'.

Richard Thaler argues that since people often fail to act rationally and in their own interests they can only benefit from being nudged in the right direction by governments, experts, advocacy organizations or businesses. Nudging does not simply mean directing people on the right road: it also implies taking measures to thwart people from acting in ways not approved by those who know best. 'To compensate for our inherent flaws, behavioural economists argue that we must be prevented from acting on our instincts', observes Wolfe.[25] The casual manner with which people's aspiration to act in accordance with their inclination is devalued, testifies to the authoritarian instincts behind *Nudge*. Sunstein and Thaler reject the label of being authoritarian, characterizing their project as 'libertarian paternalism' and claiming that their intention is to constrain people's choices through organizing society and its institutions in the way that is likely to lead to the best results. They refer to this project as 'choice architecture', which means influencing people's behaviour so that they make the right choices.

Proponents of choice architecture often delude themselves into believing that their paternalism is libertarian and that their policies are neither authoritarian nor coercive. However, the objectives adopted by choice architects are far-reaching and resemble ambitions usually associated with totalitarian regimes. Recently, the UK Deputy Prime Minister Nick Clegg casually remarked that his government's Nudge Unit 'could change the way citizens think'.[26] But since when has it been a democratic government's brief to wage an ideological crusade directed at altering its citizens' thoughts? According to this scenario, governing is not so much about realizing people's aspirations as it is about changing these aspirations so that they correspond to the worldview of choice architects.

The project of remoulding the way people think and act requires a significant erosion of people's right to assent to, or reject, policies. This approach clearly presupposes the elimination of a two-way process of discussion between citizens and their rulers. As a UK Cabinet Office Paper 'Mindspace: influencing behaviour through public policy' explains:

> MINDSPACE effects depend at least partly on automatic influences on behaviour. This means that citizens may not fully

realise that their behaviour is being changed – or, at least, how it is being changed. Therefore, there may be little opportunity for citizens to opt-out or choose otherwise; the concept of 'choice architecture' is less use here. Any action that may reduce the 'right to be wrong' is likely to be controversial.[27]

The authors of 'Mindspace' are in no doubt that their policy of choice depends on achieving objectives behind the back of the electorate. Consequently, the public 'may not fully realise' what's happening, and of course there is no 'opt-out'; citizens have no choice but to acquiesce.

The presumption of a public that is powerless to determine its future is central to the project of constraining private preference through behaviour management. The authors of 'Mindspace' put forward a fantasy where government action can be seen to augment freedom by acting as 'surrogate willpower'. A government that substitutes itself for the exercise of human free will is one for whom freedom can have little meaning. As Wolfe warns us, 'under the rules of liberal paternalism, all power goes to the choice architects'.[28]

Intolerance towards private life

The imperative of behaviour modification demands that even the most personal dimension of human experience – private communications, personal emotion and beliefs – should in principle be subject to government regulation. Consequently, the liberal model of toleration, which requires that the state refrain from interfering in the private lives of its citizens, has been called into question by policymakers and their experts. One of the principal characteristic of the New Intolerance is its renunciation of the distinction between the public and private spheres. As Gey notes, according to current censorship theory 'anything that contributes to the development of social values or political perspectives should be subject to government regulation, even if the influence occurs outside the traditional public sphere'.[29]

The call to regulate private expressions is sometimes conveyed through an explicit rejection of the liberal ethos of freedom and autonomy. This approach is systematically expressed by Catharine MacKinnon, whose contempt for the protection of privacy is grounded in the belief that privacy and autonomy, and their closely linked ideal of freedom, represent the interest of men and not women. MacKinnon takes the view that privacy allows male domination to flourish and women's oppression to be perpetuated. Since, from her perspective, the protection of privacy represents the protection of male domination, she is happy for the state to intervene and suppress pornography and other expressions of sexist behaviour. Libertarian paternalists also support the colonization of the private sphere, albeit on different grounds, as indicated by Cass Sunstein's assertion that 'a democratic government should sometimes take private preferences as an object of regulation and control'.[30]

The loss of restraint towards intervention in people's private affairs is one of the most significant developments in the sphere of public policy during the past two decades. As I argue elsewhere, governments, which have become uncertain of values and their purpose have refocused their energies towards the management of individual behaviour and the regulation of informal relationships.[31] Increasingly governments have attempted to adopt the role of protecting people from themselves and from other members of the public. In return for acknowledging the authority of government to play the role of a caring Big Brother, the state is happy to provide support and affirmation to individuals in search of recognition. Government officials occasionally react defensively when criticized for overstepping their jurisdiction. Their usual reaction is to assert that what they are doing is not promoting the 'nanny state', but attempting to 'help' or 'support' the targets of intervention. However, with the passing of time, advocates of state intrusion into private life have become more aggressive in justifying their right to manage people's behaviour. It was in this vein that former Children's Minister Margaret Hodge insisted that the government has a 'powerful' role to play in family life, arguing: 'it's not a question of whether we should intrude in family life, but how and when – and we have to constantly remain focused on our purpose: to strengthen and support families so that they can enjoy their opportunities and help provide opportunities for their children'.[32]

The rhetoric of 'support' is frequently used to justify policies that demand that people conform to the government's norms. Support rarely means assisting people to improve what they are already struggling to do; in practice, it means placing pressure on people to adopt a different course of action. 'Promote health by influencing people's attitudes to the choices they make', is how one New Labour government strategy document summarizes this point.[33] Supporting people to make choices actually means getting them to do what choice architects believe is in their best interests. In this libertarian–paternalistic vocabulary, 'informed choice' means the adoption of behaviour that enjoys the approval of government officials and experts.

The tendency to regard altering people's beliefs, attitudes and behaviour as a legitimate and key feature of governance has become widespread among policymakers. During the past decade it has led to what New Labour ministers called the 'politics of behaviour'. Governments have always tried to influence the public in order to win support for their policy objectives; but the official pursuit of the politics of behaviour is less about winning hearts and minds than it is about the management of personal behaviour, changing lifestyles rather than influencing beliefs. Once the management of people's behaviour becomes an important objective of policymaking, the most intimate dimension of people's experience becomes potentially a subject of public policy. In effect it directs government to take an interest in people's eating habits, love life, child-rearing practices, physical activities, emotional attitudes, sex lives, reflections and communications. The boundary that once separated personal life from the gaze of officialdom has become increasingly blurred. Even statements and communications made among friends can now be subject to censorship.

It is worth recalling that the very idea of toleration was developed by Locke through putting forward an eloquent case for the protection of private belief: tolerating private vices but not public ones. The concept of freedom of belief requires the existence of a protected private sphere where individuals possess the autonomy to cultivate their personality and ideas, insulated from external constraint and interference. The First Amendment to the US Constitution provides protection for free speech in part because it recognizes that private citizens need to be able to be protected from the arbitrary acts of their government. Citizens have a right to the free pursuit of a private life that is independent of the government that serves them.

A democratic society is based on the understanding that people's interests need to be respected as well as protected from the intended or unintended consequences of the actions of the state. An effective democratic constitution will contain provisions that attempt to balance the interests of citizens with their state. Even the most responsive and accountable government is likely to have institutional interests and values that are specific to itself and quite different than those held by the majority of its citizens. As Gey argues, 'many of these conflicting governmental and individual interests will relate to the most fundamental personal and social values'.[34] Individuals are often influenced by family customs, beliefs and practices that lead them to adopt forms of behaviour that contradict the attitudes of policymakers and their experts. Questions to do with individual conscience and taste often run against the grain of official thinking, and deeply held personal attitudes often make little sense to official thinking. Governments, who possess formidable resources and power, may feel tempted to force people to conform to their doctrines of individual behaviour unless the private sphere is regarded as inviolable.

From the standpoint of democratic theory, governments are elected to serve the people and to do their best to realize the wishes of the electorate. The politics of behaviour implicitly reverses this relationship, by setting out to propagate and institutionalize forms of correct attitudes and behaviour that are generated by government advisors and experts. This is a form of social engineering that is devoted to re-educating people. On certain issues – parenting, eating, health, multiculturalism – it sometimes adopts the role of a missionary, out to convert the 'savages' in an alien land. But often it is not prepared simply to leave it at preaching. The politics of behaviour uses a carrot but also wields a stick, and it clearly regards the boundary that separates public from private life as a barrier to be overcome. So, former Prime Minister Tony Blair, who at first presented his Parenting Orders initiative as not quite coercive, went on to warn that parents 'can be forced' to 'accept support and advice on how to bring discipline and rules to their child's life'.[35]

If a government were to succeed in imposing its own view

of how people should behave at home with their family and friends, the distinction between public and private life would be eliminated. But so would freedom and democracy. If the term totalitarianism is to have any meaning, it is a system where the right to possess and act on private preferences is continually tested by officialdom.

It is not surprising that the liberal idea of protecting the private sphere is now subject to serious cultural and political pressure. The contemporary forms of intolerance – therapeutic censorship, the politics of behaviour – are devoted to the task of 'eliminating the protected realm of individual privacy to facilitate the re-education of citizens'.[36] The New Intolerance is intensely preoccupied with targeting private behaviour, since from its standpoint the regulation of individual lifestyle, speech, and ideas is seen as a key function of government. As we shall see, private behaviour is also the target of non-official or freelance choice architects, otherwise best described as moral entrepreneurs.

Notes

1 Dworkin (1976), p. 23.
2 Dworkin (1996), p. 200.
3 Dworkin (1996), pp. 200–1.
4 Raz (1988), p. 158.
5 Dworkin (1993), p. 224.
6 Raz (1988), p. 155.
7 See West (1965), 'Liberty and education: John Stuart Mill's dilemma'.
8 Frank (2004), p. 1.
9 Cited in Furedi (2005a).
10 Lakoff (2004), p. 11.
11 Lippmann (1934), p. 76.
12 Kazin (1995), p. 287.

13 Delgado (1994), p. 169.
14 Gey (1996), p. 202.
15 See Hamilton and Denniss (2005), pp. 7 and 15.
16 See 'After individualism: activating the social brain', RSA Journal. Available at: www.thersa.org/fellowship/journal/archive/winter-update-2008/features/after-individualism-activating-the-social-brain (accessed 17 February 2011).
17 'After individualism', RSA Journal.
18 Sunstein (1985), p. 32.
19 Sunstein cited in Gey (1996), p. 212.
20 See Gey (1996), p. 213.
21 Gey (1996), p. 214.
22 Sunstein (2003), p. 7.
23 See Thaler and Sunstein (2008).
24 Wolfe (2009), p. 1.
25 Wolfe (2009), p. 2.
26 Cited in Wintour (2010).
27 This Cabinet Paper is available at: www.instituteforgovernment.org.uk/images/files/MINDSPACE-practical-guide.pdf
28 Wolfe (2009), p. 2.
29 Gey (1996), p. 234.
30 Cited in Gey (1996), p. 234.
31 Furedi (2005b), chapter 8.
32 Cited in '"Nanny state" minister under fire', BBC News, 26 November 2004. Available at: http://news.bbc.co.uk/2/hi/uk_news/politics/4044815.stm (accessed 17 February 2011).
33 Department of Health (2005).
34 Gey (1996), p. 242.
35 See his speech on improving parenting, 2 September 2005. Available at: http://webarchive.nationalarchives.gov.uk/+/www.number10.gov.uk/Page8123 (accessed 17 February 2011).
36 Gey (1996), p. 243.

7

The Cultivation of Intolerant Identities and the Infantilizing of Offence

Today's cultural sensibility regards the liberal attitude of tolerance and its project of liberty as far less relevant than the granting of recognition to identities and groups. The politicization of identity during the past four decades has been one of the most significant developments in public life. There are many drivers of the politicization of identity, but probably the most important factor is the difficulty that society has in giving meaning to human experience. Some modern societies are better than others at providing a web of meaning through which people make sense of the world and develop a sense of responsibility and obligation to others. However, contemporary society struggles to give concepts of right and wrong a self-conscious moral content. As noted previously, the reluctance to make judgements of value exercises great influence over our institutions. Typically, recently invented codes of conduct rely on non-moral sources, such as psychology and therapy, for their legitimacy.[1]

Today's society struggles to deal with providing an answer to the question of who we are. In the past this question was answered through the prism of a common culture, a shared view of the world, religion or political ideologies; now, society appears to possess a diminished capacity to answer fundamental existential questions. This quest for meaning has led to an unprecedented concern with the question of identity. This problem is compounded by the overall weakening of both traditional and institutional identities, which confronts people with a sense of uncertainty about how they construct their own identities. One response to these uncertainties is a constant quest for self-definition, while the other is a constant preoccupation with one's cultural identity. The politicization of identity is the outcome of an attempt to endow people's sense of themselves with a wider group validation.

Politicized identities draw their energy from giving meaning to the experiences and qualities that distinguish those who are members of the group. Frequently, meaning is gained through a narrative that emphasizes past wrongs and current threats faced by the group. The assimilation of victimization into group identity is a frequent feature of the politicization of identity, signalling the sense of insecurity and fragility. Whereas in previous times identities were built around myths of great achievement by historical heroes, today's politicized identity is more likely to focus on past suffering and the demand that society puts right past wrongs through affirming the identity of the group.

The ascendancy of identity politics is inversely proportional to the significance that society attaches to the value of individual autonomy. Identity politics and the demand for recognition directly negate the workings of individual autonomy, demanding recognition for 'what it is' rather than 'what it is trying to become'. The pursuit of individual autonomy always involves an element of self-creation, whereas the politics of recognition involves the act of choosing a ready-made identity.

The active and experimenting dimension of the pursuit of self-determination is antithetical to the commitment by identity politics to affirming a relatively fixed group consciousness. The affirmation process requires continuous cultivation and recognition through institutional practices and rituals, and the failure to affirm is invariably interpreted as an injury to a particular group's identity.

The preoccupation with group injury is one of the most visible features of identity politics. The rhetoric of victimization indicates that it is the sense of vulnerability that fuels the demand for the validation of identity, and it is the fragile character of emotion-based identities that unleashes the permanent quest for affirmation.[2] It is my belief that precisely because the quest for identity can never be fully realized that it is open to the influence of intolerant sensibilities. An insecure identity not only craves recognition, it also has difficulty dealing with challenges to itself.

Identity politics is profoundly hostile to any questions or criticisms directed at its representation of the world. Group claims about who they are, their past, and their interpretation of their experience, are presented as sacred doctrines that are beyond debate. Such claims convey the implication that those who question their version of events are showing disrespect, and even relatively restrained criticisms are likely to be dismissed as an offence to a people's culture. Those who possess a specific identity automatically claim a moral authority to make pronouncements over their way of life and their view of the world. They implicitly assume that they have a monopoly over a moral claim to their truth. That is why identity politics is spontaneously driven to embrace intolerance of those who question their cultural narrative.

Outwardly, identity politics can appear as a friend of

tolerance, continually demanding tolerance for diversity and difference. But what is meant by tolerance is non-judgementalism. In exchange for not exposing its own truth to criticism, it is prepared to be indifferent to others' identities and their representation of reality. The coexistence of intolerance towards those who question a politicized identity and an indifference to other identities' cultural claims informs the multicultural epistemology that is so prominent in public life. This epistemology presupposes that diversity also pertains to how truths are discovered and constructed, and has led to the elaboration of a methodology that insists that truths are arrived at by different methods.

The elaboration of methodological relativism or epistemological diversity provides an intellectual rationale for intolerance towards those who question or attack cultural, religious, sexual, racial, or lifestyle groups. It is based on the narrow-minded principle that only those who live a particular experience are capable of understanding or commenting on it. So, for example in the United States, some African-American intellectuals and black power activists argue that only black people have the right to write, interpret and represent black history. This understandable response to racism is sometimes justified on the spurious ground that there is a unique black or African epistemology.

The assertion of identity-based epistemology is articulated by Dwight W. Hoover in the following terms:

> In brief, the argument as presented by such writers as LeRoi Jones and Eldridge Cleaver is that the blacks in the world are forming a better community, one which rejected the sterile rationalism of western white society in favour of emotion and creativity . . . Out of this conviction came the word 'soul'

which was a product of black experience, and an emphasis upon brotherhood and community among blacks.[3]

The representation of a unique rationality of the black soul places it outside the cultural or social experience of other people. The 'black soul', like the German soul of nineteenth-century romantics, is beyond criticism. What it knows and experiences no one else can really understand. Since the ascendancy of identity politics numerous groups have taken out a patent on their souls. Their unique way of knowing becomes the validation of their monopoly over understanding their experience. Of all groups, academic feminism has the most elaborated particularist epistemology. In their reaction to a male-centred worldview, academic feminists often project a female-centred one. For many feminist writers this focus on difference extends to issues to do with basic epistemological values. From this exclusivist cultural point of view, only women can know women: according to one study of this development, by the 'late 1970s the assertion that women's history could only be legitimately written from a feminist standpoint was no longer argued; it was a settled question'.[4]

The claim that members of different identity groups have their own unique way of understanding and developing knowledge devalues the status of objectivity. It also calls into question the possibility of public debate and communication. If one group has no right to question all the truths produced by another, the celebration of difference becomes simply an apology for restraining the freedom to speak, question and criticize. The only freedom that is allowed is the freedom to affirm and the freedom to be indifferent to the failings of others. Such a 'freedom' provides identity politics with a warrant to be intolerant towards words and ideas that it does not want to hear.

The infantilization of offence

Victim identity and its institutionalization has played a significant role in legitimating the authority of the New Intolerance. Advocates of identity politics claim that images, ideas and words that insult or offend their constituents should be suppressed in order protect their constituents from psychic injury. The kind of arguments that were used to justify the banning of the *Satanic Verses* are regularly mobilized to support calls for suppressing speech. Muslim zealots are by no means the only group committed to the intolerant act of burning offensive literature: in 2006, a group of highly privileged students at Dartmouth College, a liberal US arts institution, became offended by a cartoon published in their college newspaper, which they interpreted as trivializing date rape. Their response was to gather outside the offices of *The Dartmouth* and perform the age-old ritual of intolerance – publicly burn copies of the offending newspaper.[5]

Often the exclamation 'we are offended' serves as a prelude to a demand for an apology or for some form of legal remedy. The acceptance of the argument that offensive words need to be regulated has led to a disposition towards the criminalization of criticism. It has also provided an incentive, psychological as much as material, to feel offended. Once the feeling of being offended is interpreted as a claim for redress, people are likely to respond to a growing variety of encounters with the words 'I am offended'. The incantation of these words is sufficient to foster a climate where self-censorship has become widespread. As a result, an insidious form of social intolerance is all too evident in the informal relations of everyday life. The main casualty of this informal regulation of speech is the flourishing of the public sphere, where private concerns and hopes are rarely transformed into the language of public life.

Moral autonomy involves not just self-determination but a willingness to respect others' capacity for autonomous behaviour. This requires an assumption that all the parties to a debate or dialogue have freedom to say what best expresses their inclinations and beliefs. In such conversations, the different parties do not confine their communications to a polite exchange of opinion. Precisely because they take their opinions so seriously, views will be expressed with force and will not be self-censored to spare the feelings of others. In such an exchange, some of the ideas may well cause pain but that is a small price to pay for the truth. And indeed learning to live with insults and offensive words may help individuals cultivate the inner capacities required for the conduct of an autonomous existence.

The virtues of tolerance and moral autonomy are inextricably linked. Tolerance helps to cultivate the kind of climate in which morally autonomous people can make responsible choices and feel free to express their sentiments. Liberals support the right to choose because they believe that it is only through having to make choices that people gain the maturity that is needed to conduct their private and public affairs. This was the central point made by Kant's seminal essay 'What is Enlightenment?': 'Immaturity is the inability to use one's own understanding without guidance from others'[6]. Individual maturity can only be developed if society is sufficiently permissive to allow people to make choices in line with their 'own understanding'. Kant took the view that human enlightenment, based on openness to uncertainty and new experience, provided some unprecedented opportunities for the flourishing of individual freedom. He confronted his public with what he characterized as the motto of the Enlightenment – *Sapere aude* or 'Dare to Know' – and challenged them to use their understanding.

Were he alive today, Kant would probably also invite his

readers to 'Dare to Speak' without fear of giving offence. Daring to know requires a commitment to daring to speak out, which as we noted goes against the grain of contemporary cultural sensibility. One of the most disturbing manifestations of society's estrangement from Enlightenment values is its inability to validate the Kantian ideal of maturity: as we noted previously, grown-ups are increasingly represented as biologically mature children who lack the resilience to deal with adversity, emotional distress or offensive speech. The Enlightenment model of the autonomous and responsible citizen is displaced by a more passive, disoriented individual who requires the 'support' of professionals and public institutions. As our discussion of the diseasing of speech has indicated, we are left with a regression to the condition of the immature self of the pre-Enlightenment era.

The demotion of individual autonomy is evident in relation to speech. The pathologization of hurtful and offensive words conveys a clear statement about the naturalization of the condition of linguistic vulnerability. This diagnosis of powerlessness and absence of agency assigns moral immaturity the status of a default norm. This trend is most visible in Anglo-American societies where, according to one account, in the 1980s the US Equal Employment Opportunity Commission embarked on the course of criminalizing speech in the workplace, arguing that certain forms of speech constituted sexual harassment if they created an 'intimidating, hostile, or offensive working environment'.[7] Today, such criteria have become codified across the Anglo-American world and people are regularly given warnings or punishment for using words that offend a colleague at work. But it is worth recalling that until the 1980s such unpleasant exchanges were stuff of what was called 'office politics'. It was widely recognized that although mean-spirited speech could create uncomfortable and even painful social situations, such words were not a variant of violent harm, and adults were expected to posses the capacity to deal with such unpleasant experiences. The conviction that being offended constituted a grievous form of harm took off in the 1980s. As Rauch recalls:

> In the 1980s it began to be commonplace for activists and intellectuals to conspicuously take offense. Here, there, everywhere, they were offended. People began demanding public apologies when they were offended. Organized groups – gay activists, for instance – began patrolling the presses and airwaves for offensive statements and promptly demanding apologies and retractions when they found cause for complaint.[8]

As a result of political campaigning, protection from being offended acquired the status of a right. A potent mix of linguistic and emotional vulnerability has found a powerful expression in the identity of the victim. Given the tendency to represent vulnerability as the defining feature of personhood, it is not surprising that the identity of victim enjoys formidable cultural validation. Victim identity is fluid and subjective and can emerge in virtually any social context. The victim category is not restricted to those who suffer from crime or an act of injustice: almost any misfortune can be assimilated into the perspective of victimization. And regardless of the intention of the offender, it is sufficient to feel offended to acquire the status of a victim identity.

The mere claim that someone may find a particular gesture offensive, or that an individual feels uncomfortable with a mode of behaviour, is sufficient to demand some form of protection – if not sanction. The growing use of censorship on British and American campuses is often justified on the ground that someone has found a poster or a newspaper article offensive. In late 1998, the editor of *Roar*, the student paper of King's College, London, was suspended following five complaints from students about offensive language and images used in the newspaper. According to one account of campus censorship 'it never matters what the majority of people think': if 'one person is offended by the words or images, that is enough'.[9] Fast forward to 2011 and in numerous universities, it only takes one student to indicate that they were offended by a sharp difference of opinion in a seminar for a lecturer to issue a cringing apology.

Students have become so socialized into the ethos of non-offending that by the time they get to university they are less likely to embrace the role of championing free speech than previous generations of undergraduates. In 2007, Ronald Liebowitz, president of Middlebury College in Vermont, reminded his students of the 'value of discomfort' in a liberal arts college and called on them to accept people's right to put forward disagreeable or offensive speech.[10] Unfortunately, there are far too few Liebowitzs, and far too many university administrators who regard the tolerance of unpopular speech as not worth the trouble it might cause.

The infantilization of offence is widely promoted on campuses. The term 'academic bully culture' is sometimes used to castigate practices that should be routine in an institution devoted to the free exchange of views and opinions. Criticism, sarcasm and humour are depicted as offensive because they 'belittle' or 'demean' colleagues and students, while displays of temper and passion – the normal stuff of a serious intellectual or political dispute – are attacked for making people feel uncomfortable. Even placing participants in a seminar under intellectual pressure by asking them to explain a particular point can be denounced as a form of academic bullying because it allegedly threatens an individual's self-esteem.

As a rhetorical idiom, terms like 'offensive behaviour' and 'offensive language' have become incorporated into mission statements and codes of conduct of numerous institutions. In schools, children are instructed in the importance of not giving offence. Avoiding offensive words and behaviour has assumed the character of a quasi-moral imperative used to regulate people's conduct. While its moral benefits are questionable, the regulation of offensiveness has encouraged self-censorship and institutional censorship, resulting in the closing down of discussion. 'You can't say that!' is a common refrain, which is less and less likely to be met with the response, 'why not?'

It should be noted that the term 'offensive' is not a morally coherent concept. Being offended is different to being morally outraged by a blasphemy. Moral outrage expresses a response to a widely recognized transgression, and is directed at an act of perceived immorality perpetrated against a community and its values. Being offended, by contrast, is a privatized, subjective and arbitrary response to a feeling of hurt by an individual. It is evident that offensive acts cause displeasure, anger and resentment. What is less than clear is what kind of statements and behaviours are inherently offensive. Whether a word is experienced as an insult often depends on context, and is also contingent on how the recipient of the statement feels about themselves at the time. The same statement can be experienced as an insult by one person and as a complement by another, just as the same individual can interpret a remark as an offence one day and as an unexceptional statement on another.

The feeling of being offended is also a sensibility mediated through cultural norms. Whether a particular criticism is experienced as disquieting but helpful, unnecessary and unhelpful, or as an insult, is informed by prevailing rules of conduct. If children are socialized into thinking that the validation of their self-esteem is a mandatory obligation of their teachers, they will regard questions and criticism that make them feel uncomfortable as disrespectful and offensive.

It is precisely because the term 'offensive' is so subjective and diffuse that it has acquired such significance in identity politics. The very susceptibility to the sensibility of being offended hints at unspecified past injuries that entitle the claim to recognition and validation. Its diffuse quality allows it to be deployed in virtually any context. As Barrow observes, 'once the notion of offensiveness is allowed to float free it is naturally open to interpretation across the spectrum'.[11] Since it is a matter of individual opinion whether one is offended, there is no way of questioning such a claim – making this a very simple weapon to be wielded in any verbal confrontation.

Important differences raised in public debate often get sidetracked by claims and counterclaims about who has been more offended. Competitive claims-making has become a routine occurrence, with controversial speeches made by high-profile figures often provoking shouts of 'we are offended'. Rather than arguments being an exchange and competition of views, many discussions now consist largely of the two sides trying to get each other censored. The claim that one is offended serves as a licence for evading accountability to one's argument. An offended individual in a debate is relieved of the responsibility to respond to criticism: through treating an opponent's argument as an insult, a discussion is avoided and sometimes opinions are silenced.

The elite consensus against offensive speech exemplifies how the intolerance of critical nonconformist ideas has made such a surprising comeback. Everything from universal suffrage to organ transplants, from contraception to legalized divorce, was once considered an offence to standards of public decency. Each time, the pain caused to some people proved well worth it for the gains offered to humanity as a whole. The right to be offensive is always a prerequisite for moving public debate forwards. Today, this right is considered to be unacceptable because society has adopted a much more limited view of the value of tolerance.

It is difficult to imagine how society can be genuinely open-minded and tolerant without allowing people the freedom to offend. The attempt to suppress offensive speech is the twenty-first-century equivalent of the censoring of dissident views by nineteenth- and twentieth-century authoritarian governments. Because of its arbitrary subjective character, the current restraints on offensive speech may appear as a mild and unexceptional form of policing speech. However, the threat posed by the criminalization of offensive speech should not be underestimated. This encourages a mood of hostility towards the value of tolerance and free speech, and directly contributes to the growing presence of social intolerance in public life.

It is essential to uphold the freedom to offend. As Barrow reminds us, 'people are taking offence too often and too easily', where in fact 'we also have a duty not to take offence too readily'.[12] There is something childlike about the refusal to deal with offence. Learning to live with the troublesome experiences of life – such as being slighted, overlooked, insulted and hurt – is an important feature of adult maturity. Calling attention to feeling offended is another way of saying, 'I want your sympathy' and 'You fix it!' While every human being requires the empathy of others, learning to sort out existential problems is an essential feature of moral maturity, and taking offence is often a display of immaturity. It is also a 'morally questionable' and 'very self-regarding act to take', because of the way that it betrays an obsession with self-image.[13] 'Being offended is one of the supreme self-serving acts – far more unattractive and objectionable than causing offence in most instances', writes Barrow.[14]

The most significant problem with the act of taking offence is its corrosive impact on public debate. The malign consequences of offence aversion are evident in higher education, where speech and behaviour are systematically regulated. Universities, which were once citadels of freedom of speech and thought, have been at the forefront of infantilizing offence. Some academics have internalized the imperative of not offending to the point of actively policing speech in seminar discussions. The idea that prejudice and intolerant words ought to be challenged and defeated through debate has given way to the bureaucratic procedure of silencing them through administrative means. This culture of intolerance has incited many students to opt for the childish performance of cultivating the image of a put-upon and offended victim when faced with the slightest hint of criticism or sarcasm.

There is nothing inherently wrong with the act of causing offence, especially when that is not the objective of an act of communication. The cause of communicating knowledge and truth should not be subordinated to sparing the feelings of those who might be upset by being exposed to it. There are times when a powerful and compelling argument will cause embarrassment and hurt, and as citizens committed to freedom and democracy we have a duty not to take offence. The demand for formal sanction and retribution in such circumstances represents intolerance in its current individuated form.

As Barrow explains, taking offence 'when it means treating one's personal hurt as grounds for punitive response, involves a refusal to show tolerance, to allow freedom or to play fair – for why should you be allowed to say what you want, when others are denied that right by you?'

The paradox of social intolerance

The intense sensitivity that society displays towards offensive words could appear as an enlightened etiquette devoted to maintaining a well-mannered and polite public conversation: after all, there is nothing inherently positive about being rude. Those who counsel individuals and institutions to exercise great sensitivity to the way words are used are likely to perceive their actions as a display of tolerance. As we noted previously, there are significant confusions about the meaning of toleration and it is frequently perceived as a form of polite non-judgementalism. But it is fascinating that such calls for sensitivity and gentle non-judgementalism coexist with a palpable mood of intolerance towards those who do not play the game.

According to the current elite consensus, those people who do not celebrate diversity, non-judgementalism, and recognition lack 'awareness' and are deemed not worthy of tolerance. Today's cultural elites have an ambivalent relationship to toleration, taking the view that their own values are enlightened and tolerant while those of ordinary people are not. Indeed at a time when cultural elites lack a coherent moral project, they often succeed in establishing a sense of moral authority by favourably contrasting their enlightened values with the prejudices of ordinary citizens. The tendency by government to seek to influence people's behaviour is in part motivated by the belief that its superior insights and values authorize it to influence the attitude of its moral inferiors. From this standpoint its intolerance of irrational plebeian behaviour is perceived as an enlightened form of political intervention. The Anglo-American cultural elites have little respect for the moral capacity of normal people. From time to time their sense of contempt towards those who do not share their values is exposed to public scrutiny. One of the most memorable moments in the 2008 American presidential campaign was 'Bittergate', the name given to the controversy caused by Barack Obama's speech at a fundraising event in San Francisco on 6 April. Obama was talking about his difficulty in winning over white working-class voters in the Pennsylvania primary, when he said: '[It's] not surprising they get bitter, they cling to guns or religion or antipathy to people who aren't like them or anti-immigrant sentiment or anti-trade sentiment as a way to explain their frustrations'. Obama's casual and knowing put-down of small-town folk sent a very clear message about the cultural fault line that divides America today. It also displayed the typical double standards that characterize elite attitudes towards intolerance: Obama's antipathy towards bitter small-town folk is acceptable, whereas their antipathy to 'people who aren't like them' is not.

Two years after Bittergate, it was the turn of the then British Prime Minister Gordon Brown to expose his antipathy towards ordinary people. After a walkabout in Rochdale in the spring of 2010, Brown responded to a question about immigration from 65-year-old Labour supporter, Gillian Duffy, by dismissing her to his aides as a 'bigot'. The most striking feature of this episode was the casual manner with which Brown waved aside the concerns of this Rochdale resident as simply expressions of 'bigotry': from Brown's perspective, a query about immigration is an instant marker for intolerance.

Brown's outlook is based on a deeply held elite prejudice towards people – especially the elderly – who do not tick the right cosmopolitan boxes. This attitude is not dissimilar to the attitudes of nineteenth-century do-gooders, who regarded their urban clients as white savages who had to be saved from themselves. 'The lower classes in civilised countries, like all classes in uncivilised countries, are clearly wanting in the nicer part of these feelings which, taken together, we call the *sense* of morality', wrote Walter Bagehot in 1872.[15] The language may have changed, but the sentiments Bagehot expressed over a century ago are not dissimilar to the way a significant section of the cultural oligarchy thinks about ordinary people today.

Paradoxically, it is often those who accuse old ladies of being bigots who have internalized precisely the kind of intolerance and prejudice that is usually associated with bigotry. Bigotry is generally understood as a fairly visceral impulse of hate. Rhetorically, society recognizes that hate is not a particularly enlightened sentiment, and considerable resources are devoted towards encouraging children not to hate. And yet there is a very selective attitude towards different kinds of hatred. Certain types of people and forms of behaviour cannot be hated, but it is fine to hate other kinds of people and behaviour.

Consider a comment piece by Gary Younge, published in the *Guardian* newspaper, titled: 'I hate Tories. And yes, it's tribal'.[16] At first, it is possible to imagine that the title is tongue-in-cheek and is written mainly for literary effect: indeed, Younge recognizes that his hatred is a 'gastro-intestinal and emotional response'. From time to time, many of us experience such powerful emotions and allow our hatreds and prejudices to influence our attitudes to others. But it is one thing to hate – it is another thing entirely to endow this destructive outlook with rationality and logic. That is precisely what Younge does when he argues that his hatred of the Tories is not an 'irrational response', but a reasonable reaction to what the Conservatives have done and what they stand for.

According to the *Oxford English Dictionary*, bigotry means the 'obstinate or unreasonable attachment to a belief, practice, faction, etc.; intolerance, prejudice'. The legitimation of hatred towards a mainstream political party represents a remarkable elevation of bigotry. At least Younge is prepared to admit that it is hate rather than hope that got him to the polling station. Others flatter themselves by interpreting their prejudices as an enlightened and progressive outlook, projecting their bigotry against 'them' onto the behaviour of old-age pensioners.

Intolerant elite attitudes are closely connected to the politicization of identities. Their way of life can be interpreted as an identity that is perceived as very different to 'them'. In this case, the politicization of cultural values imperceptibly merges with a distinct lifestyle creating a disposition towards social intolerance. In my travels in the United States I frequently encounter people who unthinkingly morally condemn their fellow citizens' values, emotions and faith. Indeed the politicization of the values associated with one's lifestyle appears to be one of the most distinct features of public life in the US. Some take their lifestyles so seriously that they do not simply disagree with those of a different outlook but express outright contempt and loathing towards their manners, habits and values. I am always struck by the censorious language used by otherwise very sensitive and sophisticated educated people, when I hear people associated with the so-called religious right described as 'simpletons' and 'idiots'.

According to a study carried out by Bolce and De Maio, anti-Christian fundamentalist 'perspectives are part of the ordinary language of cultural elites', and it is 'not at all that uncommon to find . . . Protestants, including Christian fundamentalists, described in major newspapers and leading magazines of opinion as "poor uneducated, and easy to command" "bible thumpers" engaged in an "assault on tolerance and pluralism"'.[17] Their study provides compelling evidence that the 'most extreme manifestations of antipathy' towards religiously conservative Christians is to be found among the 'highly educated and among seculars'.[18] No doubt the animosity of highly educated Americans towards Christian fundamentalists is rationalized as an enlightened response to religious intolerance; but their education notwithstanding, they lack the self-awareness to understand that they are no less intolerant than their religious foes.

One of the characteristic features of the so-called Culture Wars is the way that secular intolerance works as the mirror image of religious intolerance. Yet what strikes one is the passion and force with which individuals who take a different position on, say, the right to abortion or the right to bear arms, are denounced and dehumanized. It is as if people feel that their very identity, as expressed through their lifestyle, is called into question by disagreement about the environment or immigration.

The politicization of lifestyles reflects both the consolidation of identity politics and the opening-up of private life to public scrutiny. Questions about, and criticisms of, one's values are often experienced as a threat to one's lifestyle; and when people feel that their identity is threatened it is difficult to see differences of values as just that. When cultural clashes become so personal it is difficult to remain steadfastly tolerant, leading to the emergence of a climate of social intolerance.

The intolerance of politicized lifestyle is a good example

of what some call non-legal intolerance, or what Mill characterized as the 'tyranny of public opinion'. As Mendus writes, intolerance 'may flourish even in the absence of legal constraint or coercion': she states that 'one of the most crushing forms of intolerance is social disapproval, whether or not backed by legal sanction'. In other words there are 'two fronts on which intolerance may manifest itself: the legal front and the social front', and 'the attitudes of society may also serve as a signal of intolerance, whatever the legal situation'.[19]

Arguably, today it is social intolerance that represents the most significant threat, because it deprives freedom-oriented norms of cultural and intellectual support. As we note in the next chapter, the uncertainties that foster a climate of social intolerance have created an inhospitable environment for the flourishing of tolerance.

Notes

1 See Furedi (2004b).
2 See chapter 7, 'Fragile identities', in Furedi (2004b).
3 Cited in Furedi (1992).
4 Novick (1988), p. 496.
5 See Perez (2006). See the website of Foundation for Individual Rights in Education (FIRE), www.thefire.org for other examples of violation of individual freedom on American campuses.
6 See Kant (1784).
7 See discussion in Rauch (1993), p. 18.
8 Rauch (1993), p. 18.
9 See Bristow (1999).
10 For an account of this speech, see Creeley (2007).
11 Barrow (2005), p. 272.
12 Barrow (2005), p. 266.
13 Barrow (2005), p. 273.
14 Barrow (2005), p. 274.

15 Bagehot (1872), p. 117.
16 See Younge (2010).
17 See an interesting study on this subject by Bolce and De Maio (1999), p. 33.
18 Bolce and De Maio (1999), pp. 33, 54 and 55.
19 Mendus (1989), p. 3.

8

Twenty-First-Century Heresy

The preoccupation with the targeting of lifestyle and private behaviour is fuelled by a mood of confusion about fundamental moral values. Governments and experts rely on 'research' and 'evidence' to lay down the law about 'appropriate' behaviour and 'correct' speech. That is why they feel more comfortable with indicating what is 'correct' than what is 'right'. To a significant extent, the valuation of tolerance has been eroded by the lack of moral clarity that diminishes society's capacity to engage creatively with uncertainty. The relative weakening of moral clarity and authority endows contemporary intolerance with many of its distinct features. In contrast to the experience of the past, contemporary Western intolerance does not adopt a self-consciously moral form.[1] Forms of speech and behaviour tend to be diagnosed as pathologies that need to be quarantined.

Therapeutic censors are no less dangerous than their nineteenth- or twentieth-century counterparts, who silenced people on the basis that they were immoral or a threat to national security. Today, belief and speech that fall foul of the mainstream are depicted as a mental defect, a kind of virus that requires therapeutic intervention and corrective education. In our so-called secular and high-tech age, acts of heresy are represented with more morally neutral-sounding labels, and their perpetrators are called contrarians, deniers, sceptics, fundamentalists or advocates of hate. Historically, the construction of heresy required the existence of an 'authoritative political apparatus' that could give expression to orthodoxy and was 'capable of identifying heretics and effectively "managing" them'.[2] Today, there is no orthodoxy or political institution that possesses unquestioned moral authority, and the construction of heresy is typically understated.

Movements and individuals who wish to limit the practice of tolerance do not see themselves as intolerant. In their imagination, intolerance is usually associated with the behaviour of storm troopers wearing brown shirts or fundamentalist religious fanatics burning books. Intolerance in its classical form – religious bigotry, the Inquisition, authoritarian censorship, McCarthyism – is unlikely to have much appeal to those who call for banning offensive speech or behaviour. However, intolerance comes in different guises. In contemporary times, intolerance often speaks the language of care and support, and claims to protect people from exposure to negative influences, including themselves. It is also shaped by a mood of moral uncertainty and defensiveness towards those who are prepared to question the prevailing fragile elite consensus and its insecure truths. Pessimism regarding the capacity of a contestation of ideas to advance human understanding and the pursuit of the truth encourages insecurity towards the testing of views and opinions. These sentiments prevail throughout society, and the non-official sources of social intolerance are no less significant than the activities of official censors.

Heresy-hunting in the twenty-first century

Contemporary society is more comfortable with values in the plural than with a value that everyone can embrace. Instead of the truth, society prefers to lecture about 'truths'. The celebration of non-judgementalism and difference can be interpreted as a self-conscious attempt to avoid having to make moral judgements. On most issues we are free to pick and choose our beliefs and affiliations. Educators continually inform university students, especially in the social sciences and humanities, that there is no such thing as a wrong or right answer. Instead of an explicit moral code, Western society seeks to police behaviour through a diffuse rhetoric, using terms such as appropriate and inappropriate behaviour, which avoids confronting fundamental existential questions.

The absence of moral clarity encourages an illiberal climate of intolerant behaviour. In a world where moralists find it difficult to differentiate clearly between right and wrong, it is important that some kind of line is drawn between acceptable and unacceptable behaviour; and without a moral grammar, ethical guidance often has a forced and artificial character. Evil is often represented in the caricatured form of the serial killer or the paedophile. The Holocaust has been plucked out of its tragic historical context and transformed into a generic metaphor of evil, recently joined by environmental pollution as a highly visual representation of moral depravity. The very few examples of unambiguous evil – paedophilia, Holocaust, pollution – are constantly seized upon to map out acts of potential moral transgression.

Discovering new taboos is part of the job description of heresy-hunters today. Not being against the Holocaust is probably the most ritualized and institutionalized taboo operating in Western societies. Numerous countries now have laws against Holocaust denial, and in Austria this is a crime that carries a prison term of up to 10 years. Targeting Holocaust deniers is a culturally affirmed enterprise that allows politicians to occupy the moral high ground. It was for this reason that in January 2007 Brigitte Zypries, the German justice minister, demanded that Holocaust denial and wearing of Nazi symbols be outlawed across the EU.

Moral entrepreneurs embrace the Holocaust to lend legitimacy to their enterprise. They also insist that anyone who questions their version of events should be treated in a manner that is similar to those who deny the real Holocaust. 'Do Armenian citizens of France not deserve the same protection as their Jewish compatriots?' asks an advocate of criminalizing the denial of the Armenian genocide.[3] During the past two decades, the act of denial has become the most recognizable characteristic of the twenty-first-century heretic. Just as the charge of Holocaust denial serves as a moral warrant to withdraw the right to question freely a particular version of events, so the denial of claims made by fashionable causes invite censorship and intolerance. Following the precedent set by the anti-Holocaust denial laws, in October 2006 the French National Assembly passed a law that could sentence to a year's imprisonment anyone who denied the 1915 Armenian genocide.

It is a sign of the times that very few people questioned the right of the French state to pronounce which interpretation of the past is legitimate and which is a crime. Yet the implication of authorizing the state to possess the power to dictate what people should believe and what constitutes the historical truth represents a fundamental threat to freedom. The very idea of toleration evolved because far-sighted people understood that the meaning of the truth and the true religion was contested and ought to be a matter for individual reflection. From the standpoint of tolerance, truths – historical or otherwise – are discovered by independent thinking citizens learning from one another in the course of a debate, not laid down in a decree by the state.

No doubt those who deny the Holocaust personify the most backward and vile human sentiments, but banning their ideas is far more dangerous than the impact of their speech. Moreover, by signalling that society fears the claims of Holocaust deniers, it betrays its insecurity about its own ideas. By assuming the role of the censor, society betrays its own democratic principles and risks losing the moral authority of its version of events.

The transformation of the act of denial to a transcendental generic evil is shown by the ease with which its stigmatization has leaped from the realm of historic controversies surrounding acts of genocide to other areas of debate. Denial has acquired the status of a free-floating blasphemy that can attach itself to a variety of controversies. One opponent of climate change denial observes that the 'language of "climate change", "global warming", "human impacts" and "adaptation" are themselves a form of denial familiar from other forms of human right abuse'.[4] It appears that moral crusaders have become so overwhelmed with the act of denial that they no can no longer tell what a difference in opinion looks like. The rhetorical inflation of the consequences of denial is informed by the aspiration to construct a plausible ideology of evil. The term 'denial' implies that what is at stake is the status of truth, and that those who deny wilfully refuse to recognize a self-evident truth. The vilification of denial ensures that its practitioners are dispossessed of the right to have a voice.

Refusing to accept a received wisdom is often represented, not as disagreement, but as an act of denial – and with the stigmatization of denial this charge has acquired the form of

a secular blasphemy. So a book written by an author who is
sceptical of prevailing environmentalist wisdom was dismissed
with the words; 'the text employs the strategy of those, who for
example, argue that gay men aren't dying of AIDS, that Jews
weren't singled out by the Nazis for extermination, and so on'.[5]
The suggestion that there is a common strategy of denial used
in these three highly charged issues betrays the conspiratorial
imagination of heresy-hunters.

The stigmatization of denial represents the prelude for the
demand that it be censored. Take the attempt to stifle anyone
who raises doubts about the catastrophic representation of
climate change. Such sceptics are frequently stigmatized as
'global warming deniers' and their behaviour is often compared to those of anti-Semitic Holocaust deniers. Some moral
entrepreneurs advocate a policy of zero tolerance towards
their targets. 'I have very limited patience with those who
deny human responsibility for upper-atmosphere pollution and
ozone depletion', argues one crusader, before declaring that
'there is no intellectual difference between the Lomborgians
who steadfastly refuse to accept the overwhelming evidence
of human caused global warming from scientists of unquestioned reputation, and the neo-Nazi holocaust deniers'.[6] The
language used to condemn the heretic typically appeals to a
sacred authority that must not be questioned. According to
this model, 'overwhelming evidence' serves as the equivalent
of revealed religious truth and those who dare question that
new priestly caste – 'scientists of unquestioned reputation' – are
guilty of blasphemy.

Heresy-hunters who charge their opponents with 'ecological
denial' also warn that 'time for reason and reasonableness is
running short'.[7] It appears that ecological denial, or the refusal
to embrace an environmentalist worldview, is to be complicit

in the commitment of a long list of 'eco-crimes'. Those who denounce the new heresy often cannot resist the temptation of seeking to shut down discussion. 'There becomes a point in journalism where striving for balance becomes irresponsible', argues CBS reporter Scott Pelley in justification of this censorious orientation.[8]

Crusaders against denial are not merely interested in silencing their opponents. In the true tradition of heresy-hunting, they also want to inflict punishment upon those who deny the true faith. Those who deny the official consensus on the spread of AIDS are labelled 'AIDS deniers'. '[I]f Holocaust-deniers deserve to be punished, so do Aids deniers', argues one advocate of state repression, before adding that 'it is high time African governments outlawed denial of the epidemic, and prosecuted those who perpetuate misinformation about Aids or in any way undermine efforts to tackle it'.[9] A similar approach is adopted by illiberal opponents of 'climate change deniers'. One Australian journalist writes that, because 'David Irving is under arrest in Austria for Holocaust denial', perhaps 'there is a case for making climate change denial an offence' – because it is a 'crime against humanity, after all'.[10] David Roberts, a journalist for the online magazine *Grist*, would like to see global warming deniers prosecuted like Nazi war criminals. With the tone of vitriol characteristic of dogmatic inquisitors, he argues that 'we should have war crimes trials for these bastards', suggesting: 'some sort of climate Nuremberg'.[11]

The arguments used by moral entrepreneurs suggest that denial constitutes what traditional religion used to classify as sinful or dangerous ideas. A long time ago theocrats realized that the authority of their belief system would be reinforced if they insisted that 'God punishes disbelief'.[12] Disbelievers also needed to be punished because of the evil impact their blasphemy had on others. Today's inquisitors have taken on board this insight, and insist that since people need to be protected from disbelief, repression can be an act of responsible behaviour. Arthur Versluis writes in *The New Inquisitions* that the term 'heresy' derives from the Greek word *hairen*, which means 'to choose': 'A "heretic", then, is one who chooses, one who therefore exemplifies freedom of individual thought'.[13] What connects the Inquisition to the activities of heresy-hunters today is the objective of suppressing the 'crime' of freethinking.[14]

Denial and the diseasing of blasphemy

According to the *Oxford English Dictionary*, the word 'denial' connotes the act of 'asserting (of anything) to be untrue or untenable'. It is for this reason that this response has been inextricably linked to critical thought throughout the ages. Those who deny the official version of events have always faced hostility and sometimes, physical repression. Today the word 'denial' has become denuded of its radical and critical associations. In its colloquial and everyday usage, denial is often interpreted as a response driven by base and dishonest motives. The representation of denial as an act of dishonesty draws upon its psychoanalytical usage, where the act of denial is interpreted as the suppression of painful and shameful recollections and experiences. The insight provided by psychoanalysis has been transformed into a cultural characterization of certain forms of behaviour. With the ascendancy of therapy culture, one rhetorical strategy for discrediting people whose views contradict the received wisdom is to tell them that they are 'in denial'.[15]

Contemporary culture valorizes the public disclosure of emotion. It also encourages the automatic recognition and acknowledgement of the feelings of others.[16] In such circumstances the act of denial has acquired the connotation of a negative emotional response: according to one account, denial represents the refusal to recognize a 'disturbing or painful reality'.[17] Being 'in denial' is the polar opposite of acknowledging pain and other uncomfortable facts, and in an age that prides itself on the public confessional, the charge of denial conveys moral disapproval. People can be forgiven for doing drugs or drinking too much as long as they go to a 12-step recovery forum and acknowledge their deeds, but individuals who persist in remaining in a state of denial violate prevailing cultural expectations.

The very act of denial is increasingly represented as a symptom of a destructive and a dangerous personality type, or as a disease that dooms the individual to acts of destructive behaviour. Thus alcoholism is 'the disease of denial' and 'denial is the life-blood of addiction',[18] while one self-help website informs the world that the 'disease of denial kills more people every year than any other disease', adding that 'it isn't that it kills more people every year; it also maims, cripples, disables and incapacitates more people and those close to them, than anything else'.[19]

The cultural logic that associates denial with a destructive individual condition has worked to transform it into a crime that threatens those whose claims are denied. Denial is not simply a psychological attribute of an individual, but a cultural force whose effects are threat to people's well-being. In the domain of culture, denial has acquired powerful physical and existential attributes with apparently grave consequences. The criminalization of denial is most developed in the discussion of genocide. According to Gregory Stanton, the former president of Genocide Watch, denial represents the final stage in what he calls the 'eight stages of genocide', and the 'surest indicator of further genocidal massacres'.[20] From this perspective, denial is not simply a speech act but an integral dimension of the physical act of extermination.

As noted previously, the diseasing of speech conveys the implication that the emotional distress it causes may be as painful, if not more so, than physical harm. From this perspective the pain caused by denial is a particularly virulent form of hate speech, which is why it can be portrayed as uniquely grave. Elie Wiesel characterizes genocide denial as a 'double killing', since he claims it also murders the memory of the crime. The rhetorical strategy of transforming words and metaphors into weapons of mass destruction is also embraced by the environmentalist alarmist. Psychobabble about individuals in denial who cannot acknowledge the truth is mobilized to explain why the public is not always receptive to the discourse of green messages about an impending apocalypse. The Indian journalist Mihir Shah medicalizes this response, diagnosing it as 'environment denial syndrome'.[21] Others preach that 'we can intellectually accept the evidence of climate change, but we find it extremely hard to accept our responsibility for a crime of such enormity'. According to one campaigner, George Marshall, in this form denial is a fundamentally immoral deed: 'Indeed, the most powerful evidence of our denial is the failure to even recognize that there is a moral dimension with identifiable perpetrators and victims'.[22]

Targeting freethinking

Social intolerance today does not focus on one or two targets of evil. A diffuse mood of free-floating intolerance prevails, which can attach itself even to banal disputes about lifestyle-related subjects like child-rearing and health. Although disputes about multiculturalism, sexual politics, and conflict between Western liberalism and Islam make the headlines, the issue of intolerance is no less prevalent in disputes about how to live one's life. The current condemnation of drinking alcohol during pregnancy, or bottle-feeding infants, is informed by a dogmatic zeal that resembles an old-fashioned moral crusade. Take the example of the celebrity chef Jamie Oliver, who expressed his loathing for parents who did not follow his advice with the statement: 'it's kind of time to say if you're giving very young kids bottles and bottles of fizzy drink you're a fucking arsehole, you're a tosser'. This moral denunciation of the parent is only a small step from the call to compel them to adopt Oliver's instruction on how and what to feed the child.

Advocates of a variety of causes almost effortlessly make the conceptual jump from unnatural to bad and from bad to evil. But typically, moral crusaders reserve their most venomous rhetoric towards their critics. As we previously noted, this orientation was systematically displayed by medieval witch-hunters. As in the past, today's moral crusaders are uniquely intolerant of the sceptic, and anyone who dares question their message faces their wrath. In the fifteenth and sixteenth centuries sceptics also faced torture and death. During the era of the witch-hunt, anyone who questioned the existence of demonic forces could be denounced as an associate of Satan. Such was the power and influence of the mentality of the inquisition that few were prepared to question the existence of witchcraft. As a recently published study remarks, the 'threat to execute anyone who objected to the execution of a witch' had the effect of suppressing 'any kind of discussion of or objection to witch persecution for centuries'.[23]

As late as the 1920s, one demonologist sought to associate

scepticism towards the power of the demonic force of witch-craft with a dark hidden agenda. As far as he was concerned:

> [T]here persists a congeries of solid proven facts which can-not be ignored, save indeed by the purlblind prejudice of the rationalist, and cannot be accounted for, save that we recog-nize there were and are individuals, devoted to the service of evil, greedy of such emotions and experiences, rewards the thraldom of wickedness may bring.[24]

From this perspective it was not genuine doubt that motivated the behaviour of those who insisted on voicing scepticism about witchcraft. The sceptic as a devotee of evil constitutes an important character in the worldview of the inquisitor. In the late twentieth century, modern witch-hunters continued this tradition and also targeted the sceptic. During the outbreak of the Satanic ritual abuse panic in Britain in the 1980s, zealous campaigners claimed that an 'insidious and dangerous' disease was sweeping the country – incredulity in the existence of ritual abuse. According to one such account, 'this contagion takes the comforting form of sceptical and rational inquiry, and its message is comforting too: it is designed to protect "innocent family life" against a new urban myth of the Satanic abuse of children'.[25]

Crusaders against satanic abuse disparaged sceptics by insist-ing that probably the worst thing that can happen to the victim of sadistic ritual abuse is not to be believed. Patrick Casement sought to guilt-trip sceptics along the following lines.

> It may be that some accounts which are reputed to be of 'satanic' abuse are delusional, and the narrators may indeed be psychotic in some cases. But we must still face the awful

fact that if some of these accounts are true, if we do not have the courage to see the truth that may be there . . . we may tacitly be allowing these practices to continue under the cover of secrecy, supported also by the almost universal refusal to believe that they could exist.[26]

From this standpoint, those who refuse to believe accusations of satanic abuse are themselves complicit in the act of victim-ization. Denial in itself mutates into malevolent abuse.

Moral crusaders are not in the business of encouraging discussion and debate; they are in the business of closing it down. As previously noted, one consequence of this tendency has been the transformation of the debate about climate change into a moral crusade against 'deniers' and sceptics. Anyone who questions the prevailing consensus faces censure for undermining the effort to solve the problem. Such people, it is said, do not deserve to gain access to the public because they serve a nefarious cause and a hidden agenda. Numerous well-meaning believers in their cause insist that since there is no equivalence in the moral status of the arguments, the question of journalistic balance should not apply. According to one argument, since the sceptics are 'largely members of independent think tanks, often sponsored by companies with vested interests, publishing their own reports without external review' the media can safely ignore their voice.[27] Another campaigner characterizes the campaign to silence climate sceptics as a moral imperative, noting that 'if more of today's media commentators can summon up the courage to help defend the planet, even against the powerful vested interests that continue to profit from its destruction, then maybe the coming holocaust of global warming can be averted without such a deep and bitter conflict'.[28] Intolerance is thus represented as the prerequisite for saving the planet. Intolerance has always defined itself against evil, and oriented itself against the evil-doer. In contemporary society the targets of such opprobrium are people who stand in the way of moral crusaders. That is why the twenty-first-century sceptics often face the kind of condemnation that their intellectual ancestors experienced in early modern times. Fortunately, they no longer get burned at the stake. But as one defender of the right to be sceptical warned:

> Do not be misled by the fact that today hardly anyone gets killed for joining a scientific heresy. This has nothing to do with science. It has something to do with the general quality of our civilization. Heretics in science are still made to suffer from the *most severe* sanctions this relatively tolerant civilization has to offer.[29]

Contemporary attacks on scepticism are not simply an act of rhetorical excess. Nor are they direct consequence of heated disputes. Intolerance of uncertainty provides cultural validation for the stigmatization of those who question the consensus. All societies are prone to acts of intolerance, but the prevailing climate of moral uncertainty encourages the policing of free thinking. The world has changed – yet in some quarters the twenty-first-century sceptic has become the moral equivalent of the sixteenth-century heretic.

The stigmatization of scepticism

In the spring of 2010, the official Greenpeace website carried a blog written by Gene Hashmi, the communications director of its affiliate in India. Hashmi pointed his finger at sceptics who fuel 'spurious debates around false solutions' and concluded with the not-too-subtle threat: 'We know who you are. We know where you live. We know where you work. And we be many but you be few'. Welcome to a world where the term 'sceptic' has acquired the meaning traditionally associated with a Dark Age heresy.

Fearing a backlash to a statement that most readers would interpret as an incitement to violence, Greenpeace pulled the blog from its site. It defensively justified its act of self-censorship on the ground that it is very 'easy to misconstrue' the statement. However, the usage of a highly charged intemperate rhetoric has become the hallmark of the current crusade against scepticism. Zealous crusaders have no inhibitions about accusing climate change sceptics of putting forward arguments that bear an uncanny resemblance to the statements made by pro-slavery reactionaries in the nineteenth century or by Holocaust deniers.

It is truly astonishing that in an era that claims to uphold the pursuit of knowledge, freedom of speech, and scientific inquiry, the term 'sceptic' often conveys the connotation of immoral and corrupt behaviour. Yet the practice of stigmatizing scepticism is not confined to a small minority of dogmatic true believers. It now quite common for scientists, policymakers and campaigners to denounce those who do not share their beliefs as vile and contemptible sceptics. The self-help guru Deepak Chopra writes of the 'Perils of Scepticism'. John Houghton, the former head of the UK Met Office, warns of a 'dangerous mood of scepticism'. The economist Jeffrey Sachs has condemned climate sceptics as 'recycled critics of controls on tobacco and acid rain'. Climate change sceptics are typically characterized as dishonest, malevolent, greedy and corrupt. 'Environmental scepticism is a blunt weapon wielded by desperate and self-interested apologists to perpetuate an archaic system predicated on the destruction of the Earth and her communities', wrote New Zealand academic William Hipwell.[30] And it appears that scepticism leads to war: in November 2010 Herman van Rompuy, the President of the EU Council, argued that 'Euroscepticism leads to war' and ended his speech with the rallying cry, 'we have to fight the danger of the new Euroscepticism'.[31]

Scepticism has a bad name because, for the dogmatic believer, any sign of doubt, hesitation, uncertainty, questioning, even indifference, is interpreted as disbelief and a threat. In past centuries disbelief was interpreted as synonymous with atheism and the sceptic was portrayed as a moral outcast. A wide range of attitudes – denial, unbelief, questioning – were often associated with the morally corrupt and that is why the term 'sceptic' often possessed a highly charged pejorative connotation.

In fact it was the very act of questioning the received wisdom that was perceived as the real heresy by the moral crusaders targeting scepticism. In the early modern era, scepticism was frequently treated as a particularly dangerous form of anti-Christian heresy. Thomas Edwards' *Gangraena* was one of the most influential works of 'heresiography' in the seventeenth century. Published in 1646, it warned: 'first bring in Scepticism in Doctrine and loosenesse of life, and afterwards all Atheism!'[32] George Hickes in his *Two Treatises on the Christian Priesthood* (1707) wrote scathingly about the heretic who regales 'his atheist-ridden, or theist-ridden, or sceptic-ridden . . . or devil-ridden mind'.[33]

The representation of scepticism as the precursor to the spread of moral depravity was frequently promoted by nineteenth-century Christian thinkers who felt beleaguered by the spread of secular culture. 'A vague kind of scepticism or agnosticism is one of the commonest spiritual diseases in this generation', wrote John Ryle, the Anglican Bishop of Liverpool, in 1884.[34] In this Victorian form, the metaphor of moral pollution through poison and disease was frequently used to diagnose the threat of scepticism: an early precursor of the diseasing of speech that we witness today. 'In listening to the arguments of a sceptic you are breathing a poisonous atmosphere', warned the Christian author Robert Baker Girdlestone in 1865.[35]

This was an age where the uncertainties brought on by rapid change created widespread anxieties about the future. John Stuart Mill's *On Liberty* characterized Victorian England as an 'age devoid of faith, yet terrified of scepticism'.

By the end of the nineteenth century, the moral crusade against scepticism failed to capture the public imagination, as the scientific and technological revolution created conditions that were unusually hospitable to sceptical thought. The nineteenth-century English biologist Thomas Henry Huxley, who coined the term 'agnostic', argued that the 'improver of natural knowledge absolutely refuses to acknowledge authority as such' and added that 'for him scepticism is the highest of duties; blind faith the unpardonable sin'. The liberal American philosopher and educator John Dewey depicted scepticism as the 'first step on the road to philosophy'. Formally, twenty-first-century Western societies are no less committed to science than Huxley's Victorian England. Unfortunately, the climate of intolerance towards dissident ideas means that scepticism is far less valued than in Huxley's time. Yet a measure of scepticism has always been a component of tolerant thought.

What is scepticism?

Although there are numerous variants of scepticism, as a philosophical orientation it represented a challenge to the human proclivity for embracing dogma. For the ancient Greeks, scepticism was not about not believing or denying a particular proposition. The genuine sceptic rarely claims to know that a particular proposition is wrong, and therefore could not counsel disbelief. Thus scepticism meant inquiry. It was considered to be motivated by a complex range of motives, but underpinned by the belief that the truth is difficult to discover. When Socrates explained that he was the wisest man in Athens because he knew he was ignorant, he pointed to the need for understanding that one's ignorance is the point of departure for a rigorous search for the truth. It was also his way of calling for the tolerance of everyone's right to find their own way to the truth.

The defining attitude of the sceptic is the suspension of judgement. A sceptic is someone who has not decided, or is not in a position to decide. The act of suspending judgement need not mean a commitment not to judge; it can mean the postponement of judgement while the sceptic continues to inquire into the problem. Unlike doubt, which involves a negative judgement, scepticism represents a form of pre-judgement. It is opposed to dogma and the attitude of unquestioned certainty. Of course, in some cases, the suspension of judgement can represent an act of evasion, but it can be a prelude to a commitment to explore further in pursuit of clarity and truth. This is important for the development of science and essential for the flourishing of a democratic public life. There can be no freedom of thought without the right to be sceptical. This is why the current demonization of the sceptic does not simply reflect a tendency towards polemical excess but an attack on human inquiry, and a threat to the integrity of science. Unlike religious authority, science implicitly invites questioning and criticism. Science does not provide a system of belief: as Thomas Henry Huxley once declared, 'the improver of natural knowledge absolutely refuses to acknowledge authority as such', and 'for him scepticism is the highest of duties; blind faith the unpardonable sin'. That is why the UK's eminent scientific institution the Royal Society was founded on the motto *Nullius in verba*, 'On the word of no one'. The message conveyed by this statement is very clear: knowledge about the material world should be based on evidence and on its continuous re-evaluation.

Today the critical spirit embodied in the motto 'On the word of no one' is often violated by tendency to demand submission to the authority of science. The spirit of intolerance has contributed to the politicization of science, and a scientific statement is too often represented as a dogma. Consequently, claims and warnings based on science are presented as absolute truths that must not be questioned. The tendency to moralize scientific claims seeks to negate the emergence of criticism and counterclaims. For example, Al Gore has claimed that scientific evidence offers scientific, 'inconvenient' truths. Such a representation of science has more in common with the art of divination than of experimentation, offering science up as possessing a fixed, and thus unquestionable, quality. The term science is often prefixed with the definite article 'the': so Sir David Read, the former vice-president of the Royal Society, has stated that 'the science very clearly points towards the need for us all – nations, businesses and individuals – to do as much as possible, as soon as possible, to avoid the worst consequences of climate change'.[36] Unlike 'science', this new term – 'The Science' – is a deeply moralized and politicized category. Those who claim to wield the authority of The Science are really demanding unquestioning submission, of the kind of submission that heresy-hunters insisted upon centuries ago.

The trend towards the acclamation of scientific absolutes has even had an impact on the institution of peer review. Peer review is a system that subjects scientific and scholarly work to the scrutiny of other experts in the field. Ideally, it ensures that research is only approved or published when it meets the standards of scientific rigour and its findings are sound. At its best, peer review guarantees that it is disinterested science that informs public discussion and debate. When established through peer review, the authority of science helps to clarify disputes and injects into public discussion the latest findings and research.

However, in recent years, peer review has been turned into an instrument of intolerance. It is increasingly used as a form of unquestioned and unquestionable authority for settling what are, in fact, political disputes. Consequently, the findings of peer review are not simply represented as a statement about the quality of research or the status of a scientific finding, but as the foundation for far-reaching policies that affect everything from the workings of the global economy to the lifestyle of the individual. The fact that something has been peer-reviewed it often used to signify that a claim is legitimate or sacred. From this perspective, voices that lack the authority of peer review are illegitimate and deserving of scorn, while peer review provides a warrant to be heard.

The British journalist George Monbiot represents peer review as the equivalent of a holy scripture. Boasting of his encounter with an opponent who challenged him to a debate on speed cameras, he wrote that 'I accepted and floored him with a simple question' – which was, predictably, 'has he published his analysis in a peer-reviewed journal?'[37] Andrew Dessler, a climate change researcher, also sought to floor his opponent, who apparently wrote a 'denier op-ed' in the *Wall Street Journal*, by dismissing the op-ed's value on the grounds that the newspaper was not peer-reviewed. Since 'the only place' where this 'denier' can write his views is in 'non-peer-reviewed venues like conferences and press releases', he was worthy only of censorious contempt.

In 2010, the book *The Spirit Level* by Kate Pickett and Richard Wilkinson, which claimed that equal societies do better than unequal ones, became a subject of heated controversy. Numerous opponents of the book's thesis published their criticisms in the press. Some of the criticisms were rants by individuals with their own agendas, while others attempted to counter the authors' evidence with their own version of events. But what was extraordinary was Pickett and Wilkinson's reaction. They argued that because much of the criticism directed at them consisted of 'unsubstantiated claims made for political purposes', all 'future debate should take place in peer-reviewed journals'. With a wave of a hand, Pickett and Wilkinson declared that critiques that were not peer-reviewed could be silenced and ignored. In this respect case peer review is used as a form of intellectual policing, an attempt to prevent a significant section of the public from voicing its views. In effect this sacralization of peer review represents its corruption: instead of acting as a form of quality control, it is turned into a warrant for closing discussion down.

When academics devote so much energy to the task of silencing competing ideas, it becomes evident that intolerance has become a feature of intellectual life. There is no safe haven for tolerance to flourish. What is lacking is a genuine commitment to the value of the freedoms that helped the idea of tolerance gain definition and influence. Winning intellectual and moral support for genuine tolerance represents an important challenge for those committed to defending the freedoms achieved through the struggles of past centuries.

Notes

1 This is in striking contrast to the grammar of intolerance communicated by Muslim moral entrepreneurs. See the denunciation of 'libertine Western culture' and the contrast drawn with the 'purity of the Islamic Hijaab', see Inkofscholars (2002).
2 Berlinerblau (2001), pp. 334–5.
3 Atamian (2006).
4 Marshall (2001).
5 Pimm and Harvey (2001).
6 See Pollard (2004).
7 Orr (2005), p. 291.
8 Cited in Anderson and Gainor (2006), p. 5.
9 See Smyth (2006).
10 Kingston (2005).
11 Roberts (2006).
12 On this point see Weinberg (2007).
13 Versluis (2006), p. 3.
14 Versluis (2006), p. 7.
15 See Furedi (2004b).
16 Furedi (2004a).
17 Cottee (2005), p. 119.
18 'Alcoholism: the diseases of denial'. Available at: http://www.olsoncenter.com/hom/index.php?option=com_content&task=view&id=131&Itemid=31 (accessed 8 April 2011).
19 McCright 'The most deadly disease of all: denial'. Available at: http://home.hiwaay.net/~garson/05denial.html (accessed 18 February 2011).
20 Stanton (1998).
21 Shah (2006).
22 Marshall (2001).

23 See Kord (2008), p. 67.
24 Summers (1969), p. 4.
25 Dawson (1990).
26 Casement (1994), p. 24.
27 Wolff (2007).
28 Lynas (2007).
29 Feyerabend (1975).
30 See Hipwell (n.d.).
31 See Waterfield (2010).
32 Edwards (1646), p. 19.
33 Hickes (1707), p. 88.
34 See Ryle (1900), p. 433.
35 Girdlestone (1865), p. 59.
36 '"Scepticism" over climate claims', BBC News, 3 July 2007. Available at: http://news.bbc.co.uk/1/hi/6263690.stm (accessed 18 February 2011).
37 Monbiot (2007).

9

Conclusion:
Why Tolerance Matters

The various trends outlined so far – risk aversion in the management of uncertainty, the rise of a therapeutic imagination, the fossilization of identity, the diminishing of subjectivity, the expansion of the meaning of harm, the diseasing of language – reinforce one another to consolidate a cultural climate that is disposed towards intolerance. From the standpoint of governance, the most significant developments are not so much the laws that curb freedoms but the ways that the private sphere has been targeted as a legitimate site for intervention. The conviction that government knows best is replicated in everyday life by the belief held by non-governmental organizations, experts, and professional groups that they also have a privileged access to the truth and are best placed to know what is in people's best interests.

As noted in the previous chapters, there are many drivers of intolerance. But probably the most important source for the loss of authority of tolerance is the weakening of moral and intellectual certainties. It is important to note that there is no direct correlation between uncertainty and intolerance: there have been important moments in history, such as Athens in the fifth century BC, and seventeenth-century Europe,

192

when intellectual uncertainties fostered a cultural disposition *towards* tolerance. Uncertainty is mediated through cultural and intellectual influences and particularly by society's capacity to deal with the unknown. Today, intellectual uncertainties coexist with moral confusion about the capacity to know.[1]

Cynicism about truth claims in general, and pessimism about the status of knowledge has diminished the capacity and inclination to tolerate. One of the most disturbing expressions of this development is the reluctance to deal with normative issues in public life. In the absence of clarity about the values that define society, the political and cultural elites have found it difficult to engage with uncertainty. Governments have sought to bypass the challenge of uncertainty through opting for the construction of a dense network of procedures and codes of conduct to govern everyday life. Their embrace of 'choice architecture' shows a disinclination to risk leaving people to pursue their own lives. If people cannot be permitted to make choices that are deemed wrong, it is unlikely that there will be tolerance towards their beliefs, speech and behaviour. Intolerance towards risk-taking is symptomatic of a defensive and insecure cultural response to uncertainty.

Intolerance towards risk-taking is rarely linked in the public mind to other forms of intolerance.[2] Yet a life of freedom is, by definition, an open-ended experience and for that reason it is unpredictable. As I argue elsewhere, the expansion of social intolerance and regulation of people's lives do not appear as what they really are, which is an 'encroachment on individual autonomy'.[3] Risk aversion rarely expresses itself explicitly as intolerance. One reason why intolerance rarely assumes an unambiguous form is because the experience of history provides us with a very good idea of its associated dangers. Unlike in the seventeenth century, when hard-line theologians praised intolerance as the virtue of the steadfast believer, it is unlikely that any serious twenty-first-century Western commentator would have a good word to say about intolerance. Society is sensitive to the destruction and appalling loss of life brought by intolerance, which is why public institutions like schools attempt to inoculate children from its scourge by seeking to teach the importance of tolerance.

Unfortunately, while society is good at denouncing the classical symptoms of intolerance, it appears far less effective at recognizing its contemporary manifestations. Calls for the desecration of religious buildings, the burning of books, or threats to the lives of authors who offend Islam, are rightly seen as expressions of the spirit of intolerance, and artists and entertainers are often sensitive to attempts to censor their work and quick to stand up for their own free speech. However, as we have suggested throughout this book, the response to the contemporary forms of intolerance is far more ambivalent. Laws that ban speech on the grounds that it offends, or incites people to 'hatred' of specific religions, races, sexualities or lifestyles, have become enacted with virtually no opposition. Informal calls to deny sceptics the right to a voice enjoy the acquiescence of significant sections of the elite. An intensive regime of speech regulation has become the norm in public and private institutions throughout society, and not being offensive has become a new piety.

The etiquette of not offending has fostered a climate where 'minding your words' is not so much a display of polite behaviour as a form of defensive self-censorship. This illiberal sensibility extends into the domain of private life, where government initiatives designed to protect people from their own irrationality continually call into question the integrity of individual autonomy. The lack of serious opposition to government projects that target people's beliefs, attitudes and behaviour betrays the loss of valuation for real tolerance, indicating that one of the most fundamental tenets of liberty – restraining the power of the state to determine how people should live their lives – is under threat. In such circumstances it is difficult to avoid the conclusion that society's attitude towards tolerance is at best ambivalent, and that this important virtue has been emptied of meaning.

Using the wrong words will get you into trouble. As a review of free speech in the UK reminds us, 'for all the talk of freedom of speech in liberal democracies, poorly chosen comments can end careers, lead to arrest, or just cause offence and embarrassment'.[4] The coexistence of the rhetoric of tolerance with the reality of new forms of intolerance reflects society's ambivalence towards tolerance and exposes the confusions that surround its meaning. As we have noted, the dominant usage of this word has little in common with its classical meaning, serving instead as a form of bland exhortation to act with sensitivity and politeness. In such circumstances, as an introductory text on this subject indicates, 'in spite of the lack of agreement, the popularity of tolerance continues well into the twenty-first century'.[5] However, what is popular about tolerance is its recently acquired association with the current etiquette of appropriate behaviour – respect, recognition, affirmation and non-judgementalism. As an attitude promoted by current etiquette, tolerance has been turned into a disposition that can be taught in the classroom, presented as something that is 'essentially cognitive' and can be 'implemented via educational initiatives'.[6] But instructions in tolerance miss the point that this is a principle that is internalized though its practice. The habit of risk-taking and the cultivation of freedom are the results of citizens engaging with the issues of the day in public.

Contemporary rhetoric obscures the fact that many of the values that are integral to tolerance run counter to the dominant strands of twenty-first-century Anglo-American culture. One of the most important insights of the advocates of freedom and tolerance was the conviction that government should not be in the business of directing or suppressing people's beliefs. This conviction helped secure the protection of free speech in American society. As Steven Gey argues, under the liberal interpretation of the First Amendment, 'it is much easier to defend the protection of speech, because the government is robbed of its usual justifications for suppressing that speech'. Freedom of speech is truly protected when it is recognized that 'government has no authority to use its legal authority to identify and enforce any particular version of right and wrong, truth and untruth',[7] and it is when the public accepts the view that the government 'has no paternalistic role over matters of the intellect, just as it has no paternalistic role over matters of the soul' that tolerance becomes a way of life rather than a shallow gesture of acceptance.[8] Today, paternalism does not need to hide behind mystifying official rhetoric. That politicians can describe their policies as 'libertarian paternalistic' without shame or irony is symptomatic of a political climate that does not take individual autonomy and the private sphere very seriously.

Virtually every value that is integral to tolerance is negated by the cultural script that influences everyday life. Even a brief perusal of Mill's *On Liberty* is sufficient to sensitize the reader to the chasm that separates these ideals from the contemporary cultural imagination. Mill defended heretics because he recognized that through their questioning of received wisdom, they ensured that society was forced to account for its views and, if necessary, to rectify them. Now even radical countercultural critics denigrate heretics, denouncing them as 'sceptics', 'deniers' or 'contrarians' who are the servants of a nefarious hidden agenda.

Furthermore, all the key values that are bound up with tolerance are explicitly or implicitly put into question by more commanding cultural norms. Moral autonomy is called into question through the ascendancy of the identity of vulnerability. The integrity of the private sphere is constantly tested by the politics of behaviour. The representation of speech as an instrument for gaining insights into the truth faces stiff competition with the tendency to depict it as a potentially harmful and destructive weapon. Criticism and plain speaking are often countered by the charge that they are offensive and therefore traumatizing. Discrimination and judgement are directly negated by the powerful therapeutic etiquette of recognition and affirmation. Science as an open-ended journey of discovery is presented as the dogma of 'The Science'. The project of dissolving misplaced uncertainty through questioning and debate is directly countered by the current tendency to police uncertainty. Suspicion towards the threat of the state directing people's belief has declined and the acceptance of state paternalism has become widespread.

The contrast between the values necessary for the working of tolerance and those that are in vogue today are highlighted in the table below.

Tolerance	The New Intolerance
Moral autonomy	Vulnerability/identity
Valuation of private sphere	Politics of behaviour
Speech as the means to truth	Speech as a disease
Criticism as the means to clarity	Offensive speech as traumatizing
Discrimination/judgement	Recognition/affirmation

(*continued*)

Tolerance	The New Intolerance
Science as open-ended inquiry	'The Science'
Scepticism of certainty	The policing of uncertainty
Acceptance of the heretic	Pathologization of heresy
Suspicion of state direction of belief	Libertarian paternalism
Openness to risk-taking	Risk aversion

It is striking that values that have been integral to the historical evolution of tolerance have lost their commanding cultural influence. The one possible exception is the status of science as an open-ended inquiry: scientists continue to experiment and maintain an orientation towards new experience. However, important influences at work in the public sphere seek to politicize science and turn it into a dogma that can legitimize policy and close down discussion. It frequently seems as though scientific authority is replacing religious and moral authority, and in the process being transformed into a dogma. Parents are advised to adopt this or that child-rearing technique on the grounds that 'the research' has shown what is best for kids. Scientific studies are frequently used to instruct people on how to conduct their relationships and family life, what food they should eat, how much alcohol they should drink, how frequently they can expose their skin to the sun, and how they should have sex. Virtually every aspect of human life is discussed in scientific terms, and justified with reference to a piece of research or by appealing to the judgement of experts.

Despite its formidable intellectual powers, science can only provide a provisional solution to the contemporary crisis of belief. Historically, science emerged through a struggle with religious dogma. A belief in the power of science to discover how the world works should not be taken to mean that science itself is a belief. Indeed, science is an inherently sceptical enterprise, since it respects no authority other than evidence. Its critical spirit is frequently violated today by the growing tendency to treat science as a belief that provides an unquestionable account of the Truth. Indeed, it is striking that the Royal Society has dropped the phrase 'On the word of no one' from its website.[9] When science is transformed into Truth, this indicates that tolerance is in short supply.

The slippage between a scientific fact and moral exhortation is accomplished with remarkable ease in a world where people lack the confidence to speak in the language of right and wrong. But turning science into an arbiter of policy and behaviour only serves to confuse matters. Science can provide facts about the way the world works, but it cannot say very much about what it all means and what we should do about it. Yes, the search for truth requires scientific experimentation and the discovery of new facts; but it demands tolerance for its very survival.

What does tolerance mean today?

Even at the best of times, societies find it difficult to practise tolerance consistently. From its elaboration as an important principle for managing conflicts of beliefs to its gradual transformation into a liberal moral virtue all the way to the present day, the capacity to tolerate was always tested by events. Tolerance does not come naturally; it is not a sentiment that spontaneously arises in response to beliefs and lifestyles that conflict with our own. People find it difficult to resist the temptation of adopting a double standard and find some persuasive reason for not tolerating someone else's right to communicate their obnoxious views. Expressions of censorious opinion are now even justified as a necessary measure for protecting individuals and groups from the harm of intolerance – so a spokesman for a group of moderate Muslims can write thus to the British TV Channel 4, demanding that a programme featuring 'extremists' should not be shown:

> The invitation of these two extremist speakers by Channel 4 is deeply problematic. By presenting extremist views as representative of mainstream Islam, it not only reinforces negative stereotypes of Islam to non-Muslims, but it serves to legitimise these intolerant opinions within Muslim circles.[10]

As noted previously, the attitude of rationing tolerance in exchange for the dubious benefit of protecting people's fragile identity is common. Arguments that claim that tolerance for freedom of speech needs to be balanced by the need to affirm equality also exercises a significant influence in contemporary intellectual life. In this climate, hard-won freedoms and civil liberties have become negotiable. There appears to be very little resistance to the idea that private life is a commodity that should be traded for the alleged benefit of greater security. A variant of this argument presents freedom as a moral value competing with that of equality, with radical critics of free speech resting their case on the claim that they are protecting the powerless from the influence of the powerful. From this standpoint therapeutic censorship protects the weak from the words of the strong.

One of the most disturbing manifestations of intellectuals' disenchantment with tolerance is the ease with which many have internalized the belief that, because free speech can be harmful, it should be regulated to protect the weak. So a fine historical study, *Freedom of Speech in Early Stuart England*, concludes with an argument for its restriction in the current era: the author advances an argument that 'would continue to aspire to treat freedom of speech as a right constitutive of free states, but would question the elevation of free speech to the status of a principle that takes precedence over the well-being of people, or even over truth itself (as is the case with Holocaust denial)'.[11] Once the idea that freedom of speech is antithetical to the 'well-being of people' takes hold, it necessarily becomes a risky right that demands careful regulation. The belief that free speech is actually a precondition for the well-being of society, and one of the key tenets of tolerance, faces constant challenge from advocates of the diseasing of speech.

The first challenge that faces those concerned with restoring the status of the classical liberal idea of tolerance is to counter the corrosive cynicism directed at the intellectual authority of freedom. That means challenging the argument that freedom must be balanced against an equally significant value such as equality or security. Freedom and tolerance need to be upheld as virtues that are important in their own right and, if necessary, society must revisit the debates that have influenced the emergence of their development. In the first instance the arguments supporting the classical ideal of tolerance need to be restated and developed to show their continuing relevance today. To realize this objective it is necessary to recover or rehabilitate the acts of judgement and discrimination. Tolerance needs to be freed from the therapeutic cultural influences that have reduced this concept to the act of acceptance and recognition. Criticism, and even disrespect, of competing beliefs and views is entirely consistent with the act of tolerance: indeed tolerance has as its presupposition the logically prior assumption of disagreement and disapproval. Society needs to regain the capacity to question, discriminate and judge.

Before tolerance can regain its influence over public life its meaning needs to be clarified. The concept has been robbed of

any epistemological or moral significance, and turned into a
moralizing gesture of approval of group identity. The idea of
tolerance needs to be rescued from its illiberal usage in order
to harness its influence to restrain the influence of dogmatism,
social conformism, and the political influence of the state.

A tolerant society offers unconditional support for the idea
of free speech. Many people believe that on balance it is good
that most people are reluctant to express their dislike of other
people publicly, and there is a belief that policing xenophobic
or racist speech can curb the spread of the virus of hate. But
the bureaucratic shutting down of discussion does not encourage people to be more open-minded: it merely drives people's
resentment underground. The problem with censorship is not
simply that it does not work: our argument is also based on a
principled rejection of the right of the state to police people's
opinions and beliefs. Whatever benefits a community may
accrue from the silencing of hateful and xenophobic words
would come at the unacceptably high price of recognizing the
authority of the state in settling disputes about differences
of views.

One consequence of this censorious climate is that people
often feel that they lack a language through which they can
express their beliefs and judgements. Like children, who are
told to watch their words, many adults feel resentment and
frustration. That is why so many of the outbursts of dramatic
speech acts such as the rhetoric that surrounded the Danish
cartoon controversy have such an infantile quality to it. Such
outbursts of confusion are inevitable in circumstances where
there is little space for conducting an adult conversation about
competing cultural values.

A tolerant society provides an opportunity for the max-
imum freedom of action. It protects people's right to behave

in accordance with their beliefs. The only qualification on the exercise of such freedom is that it does not cause physical harm to other people. One of the requirements of the freedom to act on one's beliefs is the restraint of the juridification of everyday life. A vast network of codes of conduct and speech codes has led to the micro-policing of individual conduct, intruding into the domain of informal relations and tending to compromise the capacity to exercise individual autonomy.

A truly tolerant society cultivates the principle of individual and moral autonomy, because autonomy provides the means through which people realize their potential and character as human beings. The opportunity to act and express oneself in accordance with one's inclination, experience and reasoning allows people to develop their sense of self and to gain an understanding of where they stand in relation to their fellow human beings. It is through the ability to pursue autonomous decision making that individuals learn to take responsibility for their actions, and develop the capacity to assume a measure of responsibility for the well-being of their fellow citizens.

A tolerant society seeks to restrain the role of the state so that it does not have the opportunity to influence individual belief and private behaviour. Democracy is based on a variant of a system of popular control of government. At least in principle, it is the government that ought to be held accountable to the people and not the other way around. That means that government does not have a legitimate authority to manipulate people's beliefs and lifestyles, and nor does it have the authority to indoctrinate its citizens with its interpretation of what constitutes the ends of life. The current tendency of officials and experts to assume that they should determine how citizens should live their lives deprives people of the possibility of independent choice making. Yet as Kant remarked, Enlightenment can only be gained if society is sufficiently permissive to allow people to make choices in line with their own understanding of their circumstances.

Tolerance matters because it allows human beings a degree of influence over the unfolding of their destiny. It provides an opportunity for people to be themselves – or at least, to gain an understanding of their strengths and weaknesses. Tolerance is a virtue because it takes human beings very seriously, recognizing that without the freedom to err people can never acquire the freedom to discover truths. It is always difficult to tolerate disagreeable beliefs and customs. That is why the battle for tolerance is part of an endless struggle for freedom.

Notes

1 See my discussion on the current mood of pessimism regarding what can be known in Furedi (2007), chapter 3.
2 On a discussion of society's aversion of risk and its relation to social intolerance see Furedi (2006), chapter 6.
3 Furedi (2006), p. 163.
4 Rohrer (2010).
5 Moreno-Riano (2006), p. 1, who also adds that 'tolerance or the lack thereof dominates the current socio-political dialogue and exchange of ideas'.
6 Moreno-Riano (2006), p. 8.
7 Gey (2008), p. 21.
8 Gey (2008), p. 21.
9 See Pile and Blackman (2007).
10 See Rajab (2010).
11 Colclough (2005), p. 254.

Bibliography

Allen, J. W. (1964) *A History of Political Thought in the Sixteenth Century*. London: Methuen. First published 1928.

Alleyne, R. (2010) 'Left wing liberals are born not bred', *Daily Telegraph*, 29 October 2010.

Allport, Gordon (1954) *The Nature of Prejudice*. Reading, MA: Addison-Wesley.

Anderson, W. and Gainor, D. (2006) *Fire and Ice*. Alexandria, VA: Media Research Center.

Apel, K. (1997) 'Plurality of the good? The problem of affirmative tolerance in a multicultural society from an ethical point of view', *Ratio Juris*, vol. 10, no. 2, 199–212.

Arendt, H. (2006) *Between Past and Future*. London: Penguin.

Association of British Insurers (2010) 'Zero tolerance policy towards fraud now needed says the ABI' press release, 22 January 2010. Available at: www.abi.org.uk/Media/Releases/2010/01/Zero_tolerance_policy_towards_fraud_now_needed_says_the_ABI_.aspx (accessed 17 February 2011).

Atamian, C. (2006) 'Talking turkey about Armenian history', *Beirut Daily Star*, 31 October 2006.

Bagehot, W. (1872) *Physics and Politics*. London: Henry S. King & Co.

Balint, P. (2006) 'The practice of toleration and the attitude of tolerance', paper presented to the Australasian Political Studies Association conference, University of Newcastle, 25–27 September 2006.

Barrow, R. (2005) 'On the duty of not taking offence', *Journal of Moral Education*, vol. 34, no. 3, 265–75.

— (2007) *An Introduction to Moral Philosophy and Moral Education*. London: Routledge.

Beattie, J. R. (2004) 'Taking liberalism and religious liberty seriously: shifting our notion of toleration from Locke To Mill', *The Catholic Lawyer*, vol. 43, no. 2, 367–408.

Berlinerblau, J. (2001) 'Toward a sociology of heresy, orthodoxy, and doxa', *History of Religions*, vol. 40, no. 4, 327–51.

Bolce, L. and De Maio, G. (1999) 'Religious outlook, culture war politics and antipathy toward Christian fundamentalists', *Public Opinion Quarterly*, vol. 63, no. 1, 29–61.

Bristow, J. (1999) 'How our universities have banned free speech', *The Spectator*, 13 February 1999.

Brown, W. (1995) *States of Injury: Power and Freedom in Late Modernity*. Princeton, NJ: Princeton University Press.

— (2006) *Regulating Aversion: Tolerance in the Age of Identity and Empire.* Princeton, NJ: Princeton University Press.

Budziszewski, J. (1992) *True Tolerance: Liberalism and the Necessity of Judgment.* New Brunswick, NJ: Transaction Publishers.

— (1998) 'Tolerance and natural law', *Revue générale de droit*, vol. 29, 233–8.

Burke, P. (1998) 'Two crises of historical consciousness', *Storia della Storiografia*, vol. 33, 3–16.

Burwood, L. and Wyeth, R. (1998) 'Should school promote toleration?', *Journal of Moral Education*, vol. 27, no. 4.

Butterfield, H. (1977) 'Toleration in early modern times', *Journal of the History of Ideas*, vol. 38, no. 4, 573–84.

Caldwell, C. (2009) 'Fear masquerading as tolerance', *Prospect*, 4 May 2009. Available at: www.prospectmagazine.co.uk/2009/05/fearmasqueradingastolerance/ (accessed 17 February 2011).

Camilla, C. (2010) 'We can't just trust experts on the risk to a child', *The Times*, 11 November 2010.

Canovan, M. (1988) 'Friendship, truth and politics : Hannah Arendt and toleration', in Mendus, S. (ed.), *Justifying Toleration: Conceptual and Historical Perspectives*, pp. 177–98. Cambridge: Cambridge University Press.

Casement, P. (1994) 'The wish not to know', in V. Sinason (ed.), *Treating Survivors of Satanist Abuse*. London: Routledge.

Colclough, D. (2005) *Freedom of Speech in Early Stuart England.* Cambridge: Cambridge University Press.

Cottee, S. (2005) 'The cultural denial: Islamic terrorism and the delinquent left', *Journal of Human Rights*, vol. 4, 119–35.

Crawley, W. (2008) 'The Jewel of Medina controversy continues', *Will & Testament*, 21 October 2008. Available at: www.bbc.co.uk/blogs/ni/2008/10/the_jewel_of_medina_controvers.html (accessed 17 February 2011).

Creeley, W. (2007) 'Middlebury's president on the "value of discomfort"', FIRE, 5 June 2007. Available at: http://64.49.244.212/article/8117.html (accessed 18 February 2011).

Dawson, J. (1990) 'Vortex of evil', *New Statesman*, 5 October 1990, pp. 12–14.

Delgado, R. (1994) 'First amendment formalism is giving way to first amendment legal realism', *Harvard Civil Rights-Civil Liberties Law Review*, vol. 29, no. 1.

Department of Health (2005) *Choosing Activity: A Physical Activity Plan.* London: Department of Health. Available at: www.dh.gov.uk/prod_consum_dh/groups/dh_digitalassets/@dh/@en/documents/digitalasset/dh_4105710.pdf (accessed 17 February 2011).

Dooley, B. (1999) *The Social History of Skepticism: Experience and Doubt in Early Modern Culture.* Baltimore, MD: Johns Hopkins University Press.

Dworkin, G. (1976) 'Autonomy and behaviour control', *Hastings Center Report*, vol. 6, no. 1, 23–8.

Dworkin, R. (1993) *Life's Dominion: An Argument about Abortion and Euthanasia.* London: HarperCollins.

— (1996) *Freedom's Law: The Moral Reading of the American Constitution.* Oxford: Oxford University Press.

Edwards, D. (1988) 'Toleration and Mill's liberty of thought and discussion', in Mendus (ed.), *Justifying Toleration: Conceptual and Historical Perspectives*, pp. 87–114. Cambridge: Cambridge University Press.

Edwards, T. (1646) *Gangraena, or A Catalogue and Discovery of Many of the Errours, Heresies, Blasphemies and Pernicious Practices of the Sectaries of This Time*. London: Printed for Ralph Smith.

Feyerabend, P. (1975) 'How to defend society against science', *Radical Philosophy*, no. 11, 3–8. Available at: www.galilean-library.org/feyerabend1.html (accessed 18 February 2011).

Fiss, O. (1998) *The Irony of Free Speech*. Cambridge, MA: Harvard University Press.

Fitzgerald, G. (1999) 'Toleration or solidarity?', in S. Mendus (ed.), *The Politics of Toleration*, pp. 13–26. Edinburgh: Edinburgh University Press.

Fletcher, G. (1996) 'The instability of Tolerance', in D. Heyd (ed.), *Toleration: An Elusive Virtue*. Princeton, NJ: Princeton University Press.

Frank, T. (2004) *What's the Matter with America? The Resistible Rise of the American Right*. London: Secker & Warburg.

Fraser, N. (1998) *Social Justice in the Age of Identity Politics: redistribution, Recognition and Participation, The Tanner lectuires on Human Values*. Salt Lake City: University of Utah Press.

Fukuyama, F. (1992) *The End of History and the last Man*. London: Hamish Hamilton.

Furedi, F. (1992) *Mythical Past, Elusive Future: History and Society in an Anxious Age*. London: Pluto Press.

— (2004a) *Where Have All the Intellectuals Gone?* London: Continuum.

— (2004b) *Therapy Culture: Cultivating Vulnerability in an Uncertain Age*. London: Routledge.

— (2005a) 'From Europe to America: the populist moment has arrived', *Spiked*, 13 June 2005. Available at: www.frankfuredi.com/articles/Populist-20050613.shtml (accessed 17 February 2011).

— (2005b) *Politics of Fear: Beyond Left and Right*. London: Continuum.

— (2006) *Culture of Fear Revisited*. London: Continuum.

— (2007) *Invitation to Terror: The Expanding Empire of the Unknown*. London: Continuum.

— (2009) *Wasted: Why Education Is Not Educating*. London: Continuum.

Galeotti, A. (2002) *Toleration as Recognition*. Cambridge: Cambridge University Press.

Gey, S. G. (1996) 'The case against postmodern censorship theory', *University of Pennsylvania Law Review*, vol. 145, no. 2, 193–297.

— (2008) 'The first amendment and the dissemination of socially worthless untruths', *Florida State University Law Review*, vol. 36, no. 1.

Girdlestone, R. (1865) *The Anatomy of Scepticism*. London: William Hunt & Company.

Gouldner, A. (1965) *Enter Plato: Classical Greece and the Origins of Social Theory*. New York: Basic Books.

Griffin, L. (2010) 'Fighting the new wars of religion: the need for a tolerant first amendment', *Maine Law Review*, vol. 62, no. 1, 23–74.

Hamilton, C. and Denniss, R. (2005) *Affluenza: When Too Much is Never Enough*. Crows Nest, NSW: Allen & Unwin.

Harel, A. (1996) 'The boundaries of justifiable tolerance: a liberal perspective', in Heyd (ed.), *Toleration: An Elusive Virtue*. Princeton, NJ: Princeton University Press.

— (2010) 'The limits of tolerance in diverse societies: hate speech and political tolerance norms among youth', *Canadian Journal of Political Science*, vol. 43, no. 2, 407–32.

Haydon, G. (2006) 'On the duty of educating respect: a response to Robin Barrow', *Journal of Moral Education*, vol. 35, no. 1, 19–32.

Hazard, P. (1973) *The European Mind: 1680–1715*. Harmondsworth: Penguin. First published 1935.

Heinsohn, G. and Steiger, O. (1999) 'Birth control: the political-economic rationale behind Jean Bodin's *Demonomanie*', *Historical of Political Economy*, vol. 31, no. 3, 423–48.

Heyd, D. (ed.) (1996) *Toleration: An Elusive Virtue*. Princeton, NJ: Princeton University Press.

Hickes, G. (1707) *Two Treatises, One of the Christian Priesthood the other of the Dignity of the Episcopal Order*. London: Richard Sarre.

Hipwell, W. (n.d.) Review of *Environmental Skepticism* by Peter J. Jacques. Available at: www.ashgate.com/default. aspx?page=637&calcTitle=1&title_id=9700&edition_id=10527 (accessed 18 February 2011).

Honneth, A. (1995) *The Fragmented World of the Social: Essays in Social and Political Philosophy*. Albany, NY: State University of New York Press.

Horton, J. (1996) 'Toleration as a Virtue', in Heyd, D. (ed.), *Toleration: An Elusive Virtue*, pp. 28–43. Princeton, NJ: Princeton University Press.

Imbert, J. (2007) 'Toleration and law: historical aspects', *Ratio Juris*, vol. 10, no. 1, 13–24.

Inkofscholars (2002) 'Kuffaar libertine culture vs. purity of Islamic hijaab', Inkofscholars. Available at: www.inkofscholars.com/inkofscholars. php?file=article.php&id=40&title=Kuffaar%20Libertine%20 Culture%20vs.%20Purity%20Of%20Islamic%20Hijaab (accessed 18 February 2011).

Jowit, J. (2010) 'Ed Milliband declares war on climate change sceptics', *The Observer*, 31 January 2010. Available at: www.guardian.co.uk/ environment/2010/jan/31/ed-miliband-climate-change-scepticism (accessed 17 February 2011).

Kagan, D. (1991) *Pericles of Athens and the Birth of Democracy*. New York: The Free Press.

Kamen, H. (1967) *The Rise of Toleration*. London: Weidenfeld & Nicolson.

Kant, I. (1784) 'An Answer to the Question: What is Enlightenment?'. Originally published 12 December 1784 in *Berlinischen Monatsschrift*. Available at: www.e-text.org/text/Kant%20Immanuel%20%20-%20 What%20Is%20Enlightenment.pdf (accessed 6 April 2011).

Kazin, M. (1995) *The Populist Persuasion: An American History*. New York: Basic Books.

King, P. (1976) *Toleration*. London: George Allen & Unwin.

Kingston, M. (2005) 'Himalayan lakes disaster', *Daily Briefing*, 21 November 2005.

Klavan, A. (2008) 'What Bush and batman have in common', *Wall Street Journal*, 25 July 2008, A15.

Kord, S. (2008) 'Ancient fears and the new order: witch beliefs and physiognomy in the new age of reason', *German Life and Letters*, vol. 61, no. 1, 61–78.

Lakoff, S. (2004) *Don't Think of an Elephant: Know Your Values and Frame the Debate (A Progressive Guide to Action)*. White River Junction, VT: Chelsea Green Publishing.

Lee, O. (2001) 'Legal weapons for the weak? Democratizing the force of words in an uncivil society', *Law and Social Inquiry*, vol. 26, no. 4, 847–90.

Lippman, W. (1934) *Public Opinion*. 4th edn. New York: Macmillan.

Locke, J. (1983) *A Letter Concerning Toleration*, J. Tully (ed.). Indianapolis, IN: Hackett Publishing Company.

Lukes, S. (1997) 'Toleration and recognition', *Ratio Juris*, vol. 10, no. 2, 213–22.

Lynas, M. (2007) 'Neutrality is cowardice', *New Statesman*, 30 August 2007. Available at: www.newstatesman.com/environment/2007/08/climate-change-lynas-planet (accessed 18 February 2011).

MacKinnon, C. (1993) *Only Words*. Cambridge, MA: Harvard University Press.

Malik, K. (2008) 'Twenty years on: internalising the fatwa', *Spiked Review of Books*, 18 November 2008. Available at: www.spiked-online.com/index.php?/site/reviewofbooks_article/5954/ (accessed 17 February 2011).

Marcuse, H. (1965) 'Repressive tolerance', in R. Wolff, B. Moore and H. Marcuse, *A Critique of Pure Tolerance*. Boston, MA: Beacon Press. Available at: www.marcuse.org/herbert/pubs/60spubs/65repressivetolerance.htm (accessed 17 February 2011).

Marshall, G. (2001) 'The psychology of denial: our failure to act against climate change', *The Ecologist*, 22 September 2001. Available at: www.ecoglobe.ch/motivation/e/clim2922.htm (accessed 18 February 2011).

Matsuda, M., Lawrence C., Delgado R. and Crenshaw K. (1993) *Words That Wound: Critical Race Theory, Assaultive Speech, and the First Amendment*. Boulder, CO: Westview Press.

McCright, M. (2005) 'The most deadly disease of all: denial', MagicStream. Available at: http://home.hiwaay.net/~garson/05denial.html (accessed 18 February 2011).

Mendus, S. (1989) *Toleration and the Limits of Liberalism*. Basingstoke: Macmillan.

Mendus, S. (ed.) (1988) *Justifying Toleration: Conceptual and Historical Perspectives*. Cambridge: Cambridge University Press.

— (1999) *The Politics of Toleration*. Edinburgh: Edinburgh University Press.

Mill, J. S. (2008) *On Liberty and Other Essays*, John Gray (ed.). Oxford: Oxford University Press.

Monbiot, G. (2007) 'The anti-speed-camera campaign is built on twisted truth and junk science', *The Guardian*, 13 November 2007. Available at: www.guardian.co.uk/commentisfree/2007/nov/13/comment.transport (accessed 18 February 2011).

Moreno-Riano, G. (ed.) (2006) *Tolerance in the Twenty-First Century: Prospects and Challenges*. Lanham, MD: Lexington Books.

Mulgan, R. (1984) 'Liberty in Ancient Greece', in Z. Pelczynski and J. Gray, *Conceptions of Liberty in Political Philosophy*. New York: St. Martin's Press.

Murphy, A. (1997) 'Toleration and the liberal tradition', *Polity*, vol. 29, no. 4, 593–623.

Novick, P. (1988) *That Noble Dream: The 'Objectivity Question' and the American Historical Profession*. Cambridge: Cambridge University Press.

O'Neill, B. (2006) 'The left has been infected by the disease of intolerance', *Spiked*, 27 October 2006. Available at: www.spiked-online.com/index.php?/site/article/2031/ (accessed 17 February 2011).

Orlenius, K. (2008) 'Tolerance of intolerance: values and virtues at stake in education', *Journal of Moral Education*, vol. 37, no. 4, 467–84.

Orr, D. (2005) 'Armageddon versus extinction', *Conversation Biology*, vol. 19, no. 2, 290–2.

Parekh, B. (2006) *Hate Speech: Is There a Case for Banning?* London: IPPR.

Pearl, J. (1983) 'French Catholic demonologists and their enemies in the late sixteenth and early seventeenth centuries', *Church History*, vol. 52, no. 4, 457–67.

Perez, C. (2006) 'Offended? Overreact!', FIRE, 9 November 2006. Available at: www.thefire.org/article/7467.html (accessed 18 February 2011).

Pile, B. and Blackman, S. (2007) 'The Royal Society's "motto-morphosis"', *Spiked*, 15 May 2007. Available at: www.spiked-online.com/index.php?/site/article/3357 (accessed 18 February 2011).

Pimm, S. and Harvey, J. (2001) 'No need to worry about the future', *Nature*, 8 November 2001. Available at: www.nature.com/nature/journal/v414/n6860/full/414149a0.html (accessed 18 February 2011).

Pollard, D. (2004) 'Global warming and the crime of denial', *How to Save the World*, 7 March 2004. Available at: http://blogs.salon.com/0002007/2004/03/07.html (accessed 6 April 2011).

Prior, M. E. (1932) 'Joseph Glanvill, witchcraft, and seventeenth-century science', *Modern Philology*, vol. 30, no. 2, 167–93.

Pucci, L. (n.d.) 'Toxic words: verbal abuse can hurt you', Ezine Articles. Available at: http://ezinearticles.com/?Toxic-Words---Verbal-Abuse-Can-Hurt-You&id=1350602 (accessed 17 February 2011).

Purdy, J. (1999) *For Common Things: Irony, Trust, Commitment in America Today*. New York: Alfred A. Knopf.

Rajab, T. (2010) 'Quilliam writes open letter to UK's Channel 4', Quilliam, 29 November 2010. Available at: www.quilliamfoundation.org/index.php/component/content/article/736 (accessed 6 April 2011).

Ramadan, T. (2010) *The Quest for Meaning: Developing a Philosophy of Pluralism*. London: Allen Lane.

Raphael, D. (1988) 'The intolerable', in Mendus, S. (ed.), *Justifying Toleration: Conceptual and Historical Perspectives*, pp. 137–54. Cambridge: Cambridge University Press.

Rauch, J. (1993) *Kindly Inquisitors: The New Attacks on Free Thought*. Chicago, IL: The University of Chicago Press.

Raz, J. (1988) 'Autonomy, toleration, and the harm principle', in Mendus, S. (ed.), *Justifying Toleration: Conceptual and Historical Perspectives*, pp. 155–76. Cambridge: Cambridge University Press.

Roberts, D. (2006) 'The denial industry', *Gristmill*, 19 September 2006. Available at: http://gristmill.grist.org/print/2006/9/19/11408/1106?show_comments=no (accessed 18 February 2011).

Rohrer, F. (2010) 'What are you not allowed to say?', *BBC News Magazine*, 29 November 2010. Available at: www.bbc.co.uk/news/magazine-11845363 (accessed 18 February 2011).

Ryle, J. C. (1900) *Principles for Churchmen: A Manual of Positive Statements on Some Subjects of Controversy*. London: Chas J. Thyne.

Sabl, A. (2009) 'The last artificial virtue: Hume on toleration and its lessons', *Political Theory*, vol. 37, no. 4, 511–38.

Schneier, B. (20090 'Zero-tolerance policies', *Schneier on Security*, 3 November 2009. Available at: www.schneier.com/blog/archives/2009/11/zero-tolerance.html (accessed 17 February 2011).

Sedley, D. L. (1998) 'Sublimity and skepticism in Montaigne' *PMLA*, vol. 113, no. 5, 1079–92.

Sennett, R. (2003) *Respect: The Formation of Character in an Age of Inequality*. New York: W. W. Norton.

Shah, M. (2006) 'Environment denial syndrome', *The Hindu*, 23 May 2006.

Skinner, Q. (1984) *The Foundations of Modern Political Thought: Volume 2, The Age of Reformation*. Cambridge: Cambridge University Press.

Smyth, A. (2006) 'Denying the spread of Aids should be as harshly punished as refuting the Holocaust', *First Post*, 27 December 2006. Available at: www.thefirstpost.co.uk/5642,news-comment,news-politics,aids-denial-must-be-stopped (accessed 18 February 2011).

Stanton, G. (1998) 'The eight stages of genocide', Genocide Watch. Originally presented as a briefing paper at the US State Department in 1996. Available at: www.genocidewatch.org/aboutgenocide/8stagesofgenocide. html (accessed 18 February 2011).

Stetson, B. and Conti, J. (2005) *The Truth About Tolerance: Pluralism, Diversity and the Culture Wars*. Downers Grove, IL: InterVaristy Press.

Strossen, N. (1996) 'Hate speech and pornography: do we have to choose between freedom of speech and equality?', *Case Western Reserve Law Review*, vol. 46, 449–78.

Summers, M. (1969) *The History of Witchcraft and Demonology*. London: Routledge & Kegan Paul.

Sunstein, C. (1985) 'Interest groups in American law', *Stanford Law Review*, vol. 38, no. 1, 29–87.

— (2003) *Why Societies Need Dissent*. Cambridge, MA: Harvard University Press.

Thagard, P. (2010) *The Brain and the Meaning of Life*. Princeton, NJ: Princeton University Press.

Thaler, R. and Sunstein, C. (2008) *Nudge: Improving Decisions about Health, Wealth, and Happiness*. Ann Arbor, MI: Caravan Books.

Trevor-Roper, H. (1959) 'The general crisis of the seventeenth century', *Past & Present*, vol. 16, no. 1, 31–64.

— (1969) *The European Witch-Craze of the Sixteenth and Seventeenth Centuries*. Harmondsworth: Penguin.

— (2001) *The Crisis of the Seventeenth Century: Religion, the Reformation and Social Change*. Indianapolis, IN: Liberty Fund. First published 1967.

UNESCO (1995) *Declaration of Principles on Tolerance*, 16 November 1995. Available at: http://portal.unesco.org/en/ev.php-URL_ID=13175&URL_DO=DO_TOPIC&URL_SECTION=201.html (accessed 5 April 2011).

Urbinati, N. (2002) *Mill on Democracy: From the Athenian Polis to Representative Government*. Chicago, IL: The University of Chicago Press.

Versluis, A. (2006) *The New Inquisitions: Heretic-Hunting and the Intellectual Origins of Modern Totalitarianism*. Oxford: Oxford University Press.

Villa, D. (2001) *Socratic Citizenship*. Princeton, NJ: Princeton University Press.

Villa, D. (ed.) (2002) *The Cambridge Companion to Hannah Arendt*. Cambridge: Cambridge University Press.

Von Bergen, C. W. and Bandow, D. (2010) '"Tolerance" in HR education', *Journal of Human Resources Education*, vol. 4, no. 1. Available at: http://business.troy.edu/JHRE/Articles/PDF/4-1/39.pdf (accessed 17 February 2011).

Waldron, J. (1988) 'Locke: toleration and the rationality of persecution', in S. Mendus (ed.), *Justifying Toleration: Conceptual and Historical Perspectives*, pp. 61–86. Cambridge: Cambridge University Press.

Walzer, M. (1997) *On Toleration*. New Haven, CT: Yale University Press.

Warburton, N. (2009) *Free Speech: A Very Short Introduction*. Oxford: Oxford University Press.

Waterfield, B. (2010) 'Herman van Rompuy: "Euroscepticism leads to war"', *Daily Telegraph*, 10 November 2010. Available at: www.telegraph.co.uk/news/worldnews/europe/eu/8124189/

Herman-Van-Rompuy-Euroscepticism-leads-to-war.html (accessed 18 February 2011).

Weinberg, S. (2007) 'A deadly certitude', *Times Online*, 17 January 2007. Available at: http://entertainment.timesonline.co.uk/tol/arts_and_entertainment/the_tls/tls_selections/religion/article2305888.ece (accessed 18 February 2011).

Weissberg, R. (1998) 'The abduction of tolerance', *Society*, vol. 36, November–December, 8–14.

West, E. G. (1965) 'Liberty and education: John Stuart Mill's dilemma', *Philosophy*, vol. 40, 129–42.

Williams, B. (1996) 'Toleration: an impossible virtue?', in Heyd, D. (ed.) *Toleration: An Elusive Virtue*. Princeton, NJ: Princeton University Press.

Wintour, P. (2010) 'David Cameron's "nudge unit" aims to improve economic behaviour', *The Guardian*, 10 September 2010, p. 14.

Wolfe, A. (1998) *One Nation, After All: What Middle-Class Americans Really Think About*. New York: Penguin.

— (2009) 'All power to the choice architects: a liberal critique of libertarian paternalism', New America Foundation, 9 November 2009. Available at: www.newamerica.net/publications/policy/all_power_to_the_choice_architects (accessed 17 February 2011).

Wolff, J. (2007) 'The ethics of journalism don't work for science', *The Guardian*, 3 July 2007. Available at: www.guardian.co.uk/education/2007/jul/03/highereducation.news (accessed 18 February 2011).

Wolff, R. P. (1969) 'Beyond tolerance', in R. P. Wolff, B. Moore and H. Marcuse, *A Critique of Pure Tolerance*, pp. 3–52. Boston, MA: Beacon Press.

Wolff, R. P., Moore, B. and Marcuse, H. (1969) *A Critique of Pure Tolerance*. Boston, MA: Beacon Press.

Wood, P. (2010) 'From diversity to sustainability: how campus ideology is born', *Chronicle of Higher Education*, 3 October 2010. Available at: http://chronicle.com/article/From-Diversity-to/124773/ (accessed 17 February 2011).

World Bank (2003) 'Diversity and Tolerance Workshop: Curricula, Textbooks, and Pedagogical Practice, and the Promotion of Peace and Respect for Diversity'. Available at: http://web.worldbank.org/WBSITE/EXTERNAL/TOPICS/EXTEDUCATION/0,,contentMDK:20575893~menuPK:2644043~pagePK:64020865~piPK:51164185~theSitePK:282386,00.html (accessed 17 February 2011).

Younge, G. (2010) 'I hate Tories. And yes, it's tribal', *The Guardian*, 4 May 2010. Available at: www.guardian.co.uk/commentisfree/2010/may/04/why-i-hate-tories-david-cameron (accessed 18 February 2011).

Zaret, D. (1989) 'Religion and the rise of liberal-democratic ideology in 17th-century England', *American Sociological Review*, vol. 54, no. 2, 163–79.

Index